Northeast Foraging for Beginners

Exploring the Wild Edibles of an Enchanting Region – A Comprehensive Field Guide for Nature Enthusiasts

Table of Contents

Introduction

It's time to venture into the woods behind your house, not just for a walk, but to discover a hidden grocery store teeming with fresh, seasonal ingredients. Prepare to transform your backyard weeds into soothing teas, or whip up a gourmet meal from what you've meticulously foraged. It isn't a fantasy. It's the reality waiting to be unlocked with the knowledge of foraging.

The question is, where do you begin? Countless foraging guides exist, some full of technical jargon, others overwhelming with a vast array of plants from across the globe. Northeast Foraging for Beginners cuts through the confusion, offering a straightforward, concise, and beginner-friendly approach specifically tailored to the unique ecosystem of the Northeastern United States.

This book isn't a dusty tome for gathering cobwebs on a shelf. It's a hands-on companion designed to get you out there, exploring the wild abundance at your doorstep. Forget complex identification keys and overwhelming botanical terms. Northeast Foraging for Beginners utilizes stunning, high-quality photographs and clear, easy-to-understand descriptions, ensuring you confidently identify the edibles waiting to be discovered.

Whether you're a nature enthusiast yearning for a deeper connection with the environment, a curious cook seeking to expand your culinary repertoire with local, sustainable ingredients, or simply someone intrigued by the hidden potential of the natural world, this guide caters to you.

This book empowers you to:

- **Become a Wild Food Expert:** Learn to identify over 100 common edible and medicinal plants native to the Northeast, transforming your backyard into a treasure trove of culinary and herbal delights.

- **Embrace the Seasons:** Discover a comprehensive seasonal guide, ensuring you harvest the most flavorful and abundant wild ingredients at their peak.

- **Unlock the Secrets of Safe Foraging:** Master essential skills to confidently collect wild edibles, prioritizing safety and minimizing environmental impact.

- **Craft Delicious Meals:** Explore a collection of easy-to-follow recipes showcasing foraged ingredients' incredible versatility.

- **Embrace Natural Wellness:** Discover the potential of using readily available wild plants for natural remedies, with a strong emphasis on consulting a healthcare professional before use.

- **Join a Thriving Community:** Learn how to connect with local foraging groups and fellow enthusiasts, fostering a sense of belonging and shared passion for the natural world.

Northeast Foraging for Beginners goes beyond mere identification. It's a gateway to a more sustainable lifestyle, a deeper appreciation for the natural world, and a delicious exploration of the wild edibles waiting to be discovered right in your backyard. Are you ready to embark on this exciting adventure? Turn the page and unlock the secrets of the Northeast's wild bounty.

Chapter 1: Foraging in the Northeast: Getting Started

Prepare to venture beyond the manicured lawns and bustling streets, stepping into a world teeming with hidden potential. The Northeast, with its diverse tapestry of landscapes, offers a unique bounty waiting to be discovered. From the rugged coastlines of Maine to the verdant mountains of Vermont, the sprawling forests of New York to the sandy shores of New Jersey, this vast region is a mosaic of ecosystems, each harboring vegetative secrets.

Lush hardwood forests provide a haven for delicate mushrooms and vibrant wildflowers. Rolling meadows teem with hidden treasures, while coastal marshes offer a saline surprise. This chapter is your gateway to this hidden world, laying the foundation for your Northeast foraging adventure.

Lush hardwood forests provide a haven for delicate mushrooms and vibrant wildflowers.[1]

Here, you'll discover the remarkable diversity of the Northeastern landscape, exploring the various ecosystems that will become your foraging grounds. You'll uncover the secrets that each habitat holds. It'll pique your curiosity about the incredible edibles and medicinal plants waiting to be unearthed. So, garner a healthy dose of curiosity because your journey into Northeast foraging begins now.

The Historical Significance of Foraging

Foraging for wild food and resources is a practice with roots that stretch back to the beginnings of humankind. Prepare to travel through time to explore the fascinating story of foraging, from its role in indigenous cultures to its resurgence in modern sustainable living practices.

Foraging in Indigenous Cultures

Long before supermarkets and cultivated crops, indigenous cultures worldwide relied on foraging for their survival. Here's how:

- **In-Depth Knowledge:** Indigenous peoples learned to intricately understand local plants, their seasons, and what were sustainable harvesting practices. This knowledge was passed down through generations, ensuring the survival of these communities and a continuing respectful relationship with the environment.

- **Seasonal Feasts:** Back then, foraging played a crucial role in seasonal celebrations and rituals. The hunt for specific plants and their use became woven into the cultural fabric, connecting communities to their environment.

- **Versatile Uses:** Beyond food, foraged materials were a cornerstone of daily life. Plants provided the raw materials for clothing, shelter, tools, and medicine. The bark could be transformed into sturdy baskets, while leaves were used for roofing and bedding. The ingenuity of indigenous cultures in utilizing wild resources is a testament to their deep understanding of the natural world.

Fun Fact: The Chumash people of California, for example, didn't just rely on hunting large animals. Acorns were a staple food source, ground into flour, and elaborate storage techniques like underground granaries were developed to ensure a year-round supply.

From Hunter-Gatherers to Farmers

The development of agriculture around 12,000 years ago marked a significant shift in human history. While the ability to cultivate crops provided a more stable food source, foraging didn't disappear entirely:

- **Supplemental Source:** Even after the rise of agriculture, foraging remained a vital source of supplementary food and medicinal plants. Wild greens, berries, and mushrooms continued to provide essential vitamins and minerals, while specific plants with known healing properties were still sought after.

- **Cultural Continuity:** Many indigenous communities continued to practice traditional foraging alongside cultivating crops. This dual approach ensured a well-rounded diet and kept the connection to the land that had sustained them for generations.

- **Local Knowledge Preserved:** The knowledge of wild plants and their uses was passed down through generations, ensuring their survival even as agricultural practices gained prominence. This traditional ecological knowledge (TEK) is being rediscovered today as humans seek more eco-conscious ways of living.

Fun Fact: Wild rice, native to North America, is a prime example of this continuity. While cultivated rice eventually became a major food source, wild rice was crucial for many indigenous tribes long before its domesticated cousin arrived.

A Lost Art? Industrialization and the Decline of Foraging

The Industrial Revolution and the rise of processed foods led to a decline in foraging practices in many parts of the world:

- **Urbanization:** As people moved to cities, access to wild spaces and traditional foraging knowledge diminished. The connection to land and the skills required to identify and utilize wild resources gradually faded.

- **Focus on Convenience:** Processed and readily available food options became more popular in fast-paced lifestyles. The convenience of supermarkets overshadowed the time and effort required for foraging, leading to a disconnect from the natural world.

- **Loss of Connection:** The reliance on supermarkets for all the food needs weakened the connection between people and their local ecosystems. The ability to identify edible plants and the understanding of their role in the environment became less important in everyday life.

A Modern Renaissance

In recent years, foraging has seen a remarkable resurgence due to growing concerns about several factors:

- **Food Security and Sustainability:** Foraging is a way to connect with local food sources and reduce dependence on large-scale agriculture, which is resource-intensive and has a negative environmental impact. By identifying and using wild edibles, people can supplement their diet with fresh, seasonal ingredients while minimizing their carbon footprint.

- **Environmental Awareness:** People are becoming more conscious of the environmental impact of their food choices. Foraging encourages a closer relationship with and responsibility for the health of ecosystems.

- **Back-to-Nature Movement:** There's a growing desire to reconnect with nature, and foraging provides a unique opportunity. Stepping outside the confines of urban environments and exploring the wilderness around you offers adventure, mindfulness, and a deeper appreciation for the natural world.

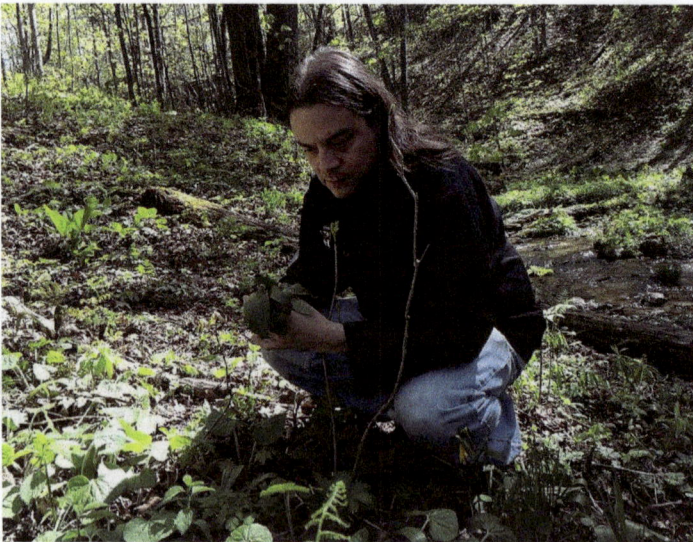

Foraging provides the opportunity to return to nature.[3]

Community-supported agriculture (CSA) programs and farmers markets have helped to spark renewed interest in local, seasonal food. Foraging takes this concept a step further, where individuals harvest their wild ingredients directly and connect with the source of their food on a deeper level.

The Future of Foraging

As people look towards the future, foraging has the potential to play a significant role in promoting a more sustainable and connected way of life:

- **Educational Tool:** Foraging can be an educational tool, particularly for children. By learning to identify wild plants and understanding their role in the ecosystem, future generations will develop a more profound respect for the natural world.
- **Community Building:** Foraging groups and educational programs encourage community and shared passion for nature. Learning from experienced foragers and connecting with others who share your interests enriches the experience and makes it more enjoyable.
- **Empowerment:** Identifying and utilizing wild resources empowers people to be more involved in food choices.

Many restaurants include foraged ingredients in their menus, showcasing wild edibles' versatility and unusual flavors. This trend highlights the growing appreciation for local, seasonal, and sustainable food practices.

The history of foraging is a testament to its enduring importance. From its role in the survival of indigenous cultures to its potential for a more sustainable future, foraging offers a unique connection to nature, a delicious exploration of wild flavors, and a valuable skill for anyone interested in a more mindful and self-sufficient way of life.

A Northeast Forager's Paradise

With its breathtaking landscapes and diverse ecosystems, the Northeast is a forager's paradise. Each region has its own character and hidden world of edible treasures, from the rugged coastlines to the grassy mountains. Prepare for a virtual journey through these enchanting landscapes, getting a glimpse of the potential harvest that awaits you:

Mountains: Hearty Edibles

Towering mountains, with their cool, crisp air and ever-changing vistas, offer a memorable foraging experience:

- **Forest Floor Treasures:** Look for fiddleheads unfurling in the spring, plump morels hiding amongst the fallen leaves, and chanterelle mushrooms peeking through the damp soil.

- **Berry Bonanza:** As summer unfolds, discover patches of sweet blueberries, tart raspberries, and juicy blackberries nestled amongst the greenery.

- **Herbal Bounty:** Mountain meadows are often home to fragrant herbs like wild thyme, oregano, and mint, adding a touch of nature's essence to your dishes.

Fun Fact: Maple sugaring, a traditional practice in the Northeast, utilizes the sap of sugar maple trees. While not technically foraging, it highlights the potential of this region to provide delicious natural resources.

Forests: A Symphony of Flavors

Lush forests, teeming with life and dappled sunlight, offer a cornucopia of edible delights:

- **Spring Delights:** In the early days of spring, keep an eye out for jewel-toned violet ramps (wild leeks) with their pungent aroma and delicate flavor on the forest floor.

- **Fungal Feast:** As the season progresses, a variety of mushrooms emerge, from the prized porcini and chanterelles to the delicate oyster mushrooms clinging to tree trunks.

- **Nutty Treasures:** Fall brings crops of nuts, with hazelnuts hidden amongst fallen leaves and acorns waiting to be transformed into delicious flour.

Fun Fact: Acorns were a staple food source for many indigenous cultures in the Northeast. With proper processing, they are ground into nutritious flour and used for baking or thickening soups.

Coastlines: A Salty Surprise

The Northeast's dramatic coastlines offer a seaside foraging experience, with hidden gems amongst the dunes and tidal pools:

- **Ocean Greens:** During low tide, explore the rocky shores for sea lettuce, a green seaweed with a surprisingly mild flavor.

- **Salty Succulents:** Look for samphire, a succulent plant that thrives in salt marshes, adding a briny touch to your culinary creations.

- **Shelling Surprise:** Depending on location, you might be lucky enough to discover littleneck clams or mussels clinging to the rocks, offering a taste of the sea.

Fun Fact: Beach plums, small and tart, grow wild along the Northeast coast. While not everyone enjoys their flavor, they can be transformed into delicious jams, jellies, or syrups.

Beach plums grow wild along the Northeast coast.'

Meadows: A Buffet of Wild Herbs

Bathed in sunshine and buzzing with life, meadows are a haven for fragrant and flavorful wild herbs:

- **Spring Symphony:** In early spring, discover dandelions with their bright yellow flowers, tender greens, and wild violets, which add a pop of color to the landscape.

- **Summer Scents:** As the days lengthen, meadows blossom with fragrant herbs like chamomile, yarrow, and wild bergamot, perfect for soothing teas or adding a touch of botanical flair to your dishes.
- **Autumnal Delights:** Fall brings a new wave of possibilities, with chickweed providing a surprising source of vitamin C and clover blossoms adding a touch of sweetness to salads.

Fun Fact: Dandelions, often considered a pesky weed, are a forager's delight. The entire plant, from the roots to the flowers, is edible and can be used in various ways. The roots are roasted and used as a coffee substitute, while the leaves are added to salads or cooked like spinach.

Beyond the Forest Floor: Hidden Delights

The Northeast's bounty extends beyond the typical forest floor, offering a surprising variety of edible delights:

- **Urban Adventures:** Even cityscapes have edible treasures. Parks and neglected corners might hide dandelion greens, wild violets, or even fruit trees laden with neglected apples or pears. Check local regulations before foraging in public spaces.
- **Backyard Bonanza:** Your backyard might be teeming with potential. Look for clover in the lawn, dandelions pushing through cracks in the pavement, or even wild strawberries tucked away in a shady corner. Identify any plants carefully before consuming them.
- **Seasonal Surprises:** Keep your eyes peeled throughout the year. From springtime fiddleheads to fall's abundant mushrooms and winter's jewel-toned rose hips, each season offers its unique bounty waiting to be discovered.

Fun Fact: Elderflowers, delicate and fragrant, are a springtime treat. While the berries should be avoided raw, the blossoms can be used to make syrups and jams or infused into tasty floral beverages.

This glimpse into the Northeast's enchanting landscapes is a mere appetizer. As you explore foraging deeper, you'll discover a treasure trove of edible delights waiting to be unearthed. With each successful find, you'll enrich your diet with fresh, seasonal ingredients and forge a deeper connection with the natural world around you.

Practical Tips for Novices

The Northeast is brimming with exciting possibilities. However, venturing into this area requires a foundation in safety and responsible practices. Here are some essential tips for beginners to ensure your foraging adventures are rewarding, safe, and enjoyable:

Cultivating Your Plant Identification Skills

Before you even consider harvesting, sharpening up your plant identification skills is paramount. It ensures you only collect the correct edibles and avoid any poisonous look-alikes:

- **Multiple Resources:** Don't rely solely on pictures in a single guide. Utilize a combination of reliable field guides, online resources from reputable institutions (like universities or botanical gardens), and consultations with experienced foragers. Look for foragers familiar with your specific region, as plant life varies depending on microclimates and local ecosystems.

- **Focus on Details:** Pay close attention to all plant parts, including the leaves, stems, flowers, and root structure. Subtle variations are the key to distinguishing between edible and toxic look-alikes. Observe things like leaf arrangement, vein patterns, hairs or thorns, and even the plant's scent. Take detailed notes and sketches in your foraging journal to solidify your learning.

- **Seasonal Variations:** Plants change throughout the year. Learn to recognize the plant at different stages of its growth cycle, from its tender spring shoots to its mature flowering form. Some plants are only edible during specific time windows, so understanding these seasonal variations is crucial.

While some foragers recommend the "hair on the wrist" trick, where you rub a suspect plant on your bare wrist to see if it irritates your skin, this is not a foolproof method and should never be the sole means of identification. Many plants cause skin irritation but are perfectly safe to consume, and some hazardous toxins might not produce any immediate reaction.

Invest in Quality Field Guides

Reliable field guides are your essential companions in foraging. Here's what to look for when selecting them:

- **Regional Focus:** Choose guides specifically tailored to the Northeastern region. These will provide accurate information on the plants native to your area, ensuring you're not relying on descriptions of look-alikes that might not exist in your local ecosystem.

- **Detailed Descriptions:** Choose guides with thorough descriptions, including high-quality photographs highlighting the key identifying features of each plant. Look for close-up shots of leaves, stems, flowers, and roots, along with pictures showcasing the plant at various stages of growth.

- **User-Friendly Layout:** A clear and organized layout makes it easier to navigate the guide and quickly locate the information you need in the field. Consider features like waterproof or wipeable pages for outdoor use and a spiral-bound format that allows the book to lay flat for easy reference.

Some field guides even utilize dichotomous keys, a step-by-step identification process based on yes or no questions about specific plant characteristics. It's a helpful tool for beginners, but using it with other identification methods, like studying detailed descriptions and photographs, is vital.

Here are some quality field guides for Beginners:

- **Northeast Foraging: 120 Wild and Flavorful Edibles from Beach Plums to Wineberries by Leda Meredith:** This is a great first book focusing on the Northeast region with clear descriptions, beautiful photos, and a seasonal guide for planning your forages.

- **A Field Guide to Edible Wild Plants: Eastern and Central North America (Peterson Field Guide Series) by Lee Allen Peterson:** This classic guide is a great starting point for beginners, covering a wide range of edible plants across Eastern and Central North America. It includes detailed descriptions, illustrations, and habitat information.

Workshops and Educational Resources

Look for additional learning resources beyond field guides:

- **Foraging Workshops:** Consider attending workshops led by experienced foragers. These hands-on experiences allow you to learn directly from those who have tested their skills in the field.

Look for workshops offered by local environmental organizations, botanical gardens, or foraging clubs in your area.

- **Online Courses:** Online courses and educational resources offer a wealth of information on plant identification, safe harvesting practices, and ethical foraging principles. Universities, botanical gardens, and online learning platforms often have courses specifically designed for beginner foragers.

- **Botanical Gardens:** Many botanical gardens run educational programs and have resources on local flora. These are a great way to familiarize yourself with native plants in a controlled setting, where you learn about edible and non-edible species side-by-side with the guidance of experienced staff or volunteers.

Below is a list of reputable resources focusing on Northeast foraging. These resources offer identification tools, recipes, information on sustainable practices, and news about wild edibles in the region.

Local Foraging Organizations:

- **Maine Organic Farmers and Gardeners Association (MOFGA):** They offer foraging workshops and educational events throughout Maine. Contact: https://www.mofga.org/

- **New Hampshire Mycological Society:** Focused on wild mushrooms, they host talks, workshops, and forays (guided outdoor mushroom hunts) in New Hampshire. Contact: https://thegardeningdad.com/new-hampshire-mushroom-society-club-reference-guide/

- **The Vermont Herbal Network:** Provides educational programs and resources on herbal medicine, including wild plant identification and foraging workshops. Contact: https://vtherbcenter.org/

- **Massachusetts Audubon Society:** Offers various outdoor programs, including foraging walks and workshops led by naturalists. Find your local chapter: https://www.massaudubon.org/

Online Workshop Platforms:

- **Eventbrite:** Search for "foraging workshops" or "wild edibles workshops" in your Northeast city or region. https://www.eventbrite.com/

- **Meetup:** Join a local foraging group through Meetup to discover workshops, events, and discussions. https://www.meetup.com/

Websites:

- Maine Primitive Skills School (https://primordialskills.com/collections)
- The Mushroom Forager (https://www.themushroomforager.com/)
- Foraging RI (https://eattheplanet.org/foraging-tours-and-classes-in-rhode-island/)

Citizen science projects often involve collecting data on local plant life. Participating in such projects can be fun and an educational way to contribute to scientific research while learning about local flora. These projects might partner with universities or environmental organizations and often involve collecting data through mobile apps or online platforms.

Start Slow and Focus on Easy-to-Identify Plants

As a beginner, it's wise to start slowly and focus on a few easily identifiable plants:

- **Common Edibles:** Begin with readily available and easily recognized plants like dandelions, violets, or clover. These are widely documented and have distinct characteristics that make them easy to distinguish from toxic look-alikes. Once you've mastered these, gradually expand your repertoire as your confidence and identification skills grow.

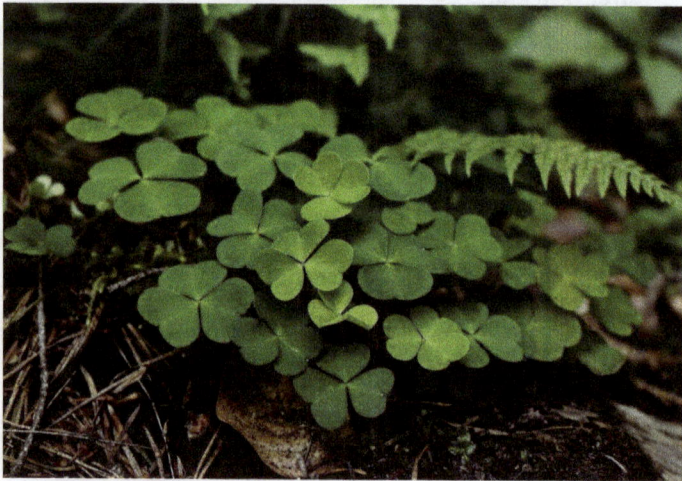

Clover is an edible and easily recognizable plant.'

- **Focus on Basics:** Many common weeds growing in your backyard or local park might be edible. Dandelions, for example, offer a surprising bounty. The leaves are used in salads, the roots are roasted for a coffee substitute, and the flowers are transformed into jams or jellies.

When in Doubt, Leave It Out

The most important rule of foraging is to prioritize safety above all else. If you're unsure about the identity of a plant, err on the side of caution and leave it where it is:

- **Double and Triple Check:** Never rely solely on one source of identification. Consult multiple field guides and online resources, and if possible, look for confirmation from an experienced forager before consuming any wild plant.
- **Beware of Look-alikes:** Many edible plants have poisonous look-alikes that are deceptively similar. Learn to recognize the subtle differences distinguishing safe edibles from dangerous doppelgangers.
- **Never Experiment:** Never taste or ingest any wild plant unless you are 100% certain of its identification. There's no room for experimentation when dealing with potentially toxic plants.

Some poisonous plants are deadly even in minute quantities. By prioritizing safety and practicing responsible identification, you'll ensure your foraging adventures are rewarding, enjoyable, and risk-free. These practical tips and other reliable resources will make you a confident and responsible Northeast forager. Knowledge is power; the more you learn, the safer you'll be exploring the incredible bounty of wild edibles in your backyard and beyond.

Responsible Foraging for a Sustainable Future

The Northeast's diverse ecosystems contain a treasure trove of wild edibles. However, with this exploration comes the responsibility to tread lightly and ensure your foraging practices are sustainable and environmentally respectful. Here are some key ethical considerations to keep in mind:

Leave No Trace

Foraging should be a positive experience for both you and the ecosystem. Here's how to minimize your impact:

- **Tread Lightly:** Stay on designated trails to avoid trampling delicate vegetation. Be mindful of your movements and avoid disturbing wildlife. Pack out all your trash, including food scraps and used tissues. Respect the natural beauty of your surroundings and leave them pristine for future generations.

- **Leave It Better Than You Found:** Consider going beyond simply packing up your trash. If you see litter or debris on your foraging journey, collect it and dispose of it properly. This small act will make a big difference in preserving the natural beauty of your local foraging grounds.

- **Respect Private Property:** Always seek permission before foraging on private land. Many landowners might be happy to share their bounty, but getting the go-ahead before venturing onto private property is essential. You might even be able to establish a mutually beneficial relationship with a landowner, offering to help with weeding or invasive species removal in exchange for permission to harvest a portion of the wild edibles.

Fun Fact: The "Leave No Trace" principles were initially developed for backpackers and campers but are equally applicable to foraging. By following these guidelines, you ensure your enjoyment of the outdoors doesn't come at the expense of the environment.

Sustainable Harvesting

Only take what you need and allow the ecosystem to thrive. Here's how to ensure sustainable harvesting:

- **One-Third Rule:** Never harvest more than one-third of the plant population you're collecting. It allows the remaining plants to reproduce and ensure the continued abundance of the species.

- **Respect the Seasons:** Forage only when plants are at their peak and avoid harvesting immature specimens or those nearing the end of their life cycle. It allows the plants to complete their reproductive cycle and ensures a bountiful harvest for future seasons.

- **Take Only What You Can Use:** Don't harvest more than you can realistically use. Over-harvesting disrupts the ecosystem's delicate balance and leaves little for others to enjoy. Consider drying, freezing, or preserving your extra forage to enjoy throughout the year, but avoid stockpiling more than you can use.

Some wild edibles, like ramps (wild leeks), are particularly vulnerable to overharvesting due to their slow growth rates. Following sustainable harvesting practices ensures these delicacies remain available for future foragers.

Be Aware of Local Regulations

Before venturing out, familiarize yourself with any local regulations regarding foraging:

- **Protected Species:** Local or state regulations might protect certain plants or mushrooms. Be aware of these restrictions and avoid harvesting any species on the protected list.

- **Seasonal Restrictions:** Some areas might have seasonal restrictions on foraging specific plants or mushrooms. These restrictions are often put in place to protect vulnerable species during critical points in their life cycle, such as during their reproductive stages.

- **Respect Public Land Boundaries:** There might be designated areas within parks or public lands where foraging is prohibited. Always check signage and respect any restrictions. They have probably been implemented to protect sensitive habitats or specific plant communities.

Many state and local governments provide downloadable resources or online databases outlining protected plant and wildlife species. Familiarizing yourself with these resources before you start foraging is essential for responsible practice. Some government agencies or park authorities might offer educational programs or workshops specifically focused on foraging regulations and sustainable harvesting practices within their jurisdiction. Consider attending one of these programs to ensure your foraging activities comply with local laws.

Understanding Plant Ecology

The more you understand about plant ecology, the better equipped you'll be to make responsible choices:

- **Habitat Awareness:** Pay attention to the type of plants growing together in a particular area. Certain plants thrive in specific habitats, and understanding these relationships will help you identify edible species while respecting the overall ecological balance. For example, certain mushrooms might have a symbiotic relationship with specific tree species. By understanding these relationships, you'll avoid disrupting the ecosystem's delicate balance by harvesting from these areas.

Be mindful of the pollinators when you're harvesting flowers.[5]

- **The Importance of Pollinators:** Many wild plants, such as bees and butterflies, play a crucial role in supporting pollinators. Be mindful of harvesting flowers in full bloom. Consider focusing on harvesting flowers that are past their peak or collecting seeds for future propagation.

Fun Fact: Dandelions are frequently considered a nuisance but are a vital food source for pollinators like bees and butterflies in the early spring. By waiting until they've gone to seed before collecting the leaves, you can enjoy this delicious and nutritious green while still supporting the local pollinator population.

Giving Back to the Ecosystem

Foraging is a way to connect with nature and become more responsible for the environment:

- **Citizen Science:** Many organizations encourage citizen science projects that involve collecting data on local plant life. Participating in such projects is a fun and educational way to contribute to scientific research while learning about local flora.

These projects might involve collecting data through mobile apps or online platforms and are a great way to give back to the scientific community while deepening your understanding of the ecosystems you explore.

- **Plant Propagation:** Consider sprouting seeds or taking cuttings from wild plants to cultivate in your garden. It ensures a sustainable source of your favorite edibles, helps to conserve these species, and responsibly spreads their presence. Research propagation techniques specific to the plants you're interested in cultivating.

- **Leave No Trace But Make a Positive Impact:** While the "Leave No Trace" principles emphasize minimizing your impact, you can also go a step further. Consider volunteering with local conservation organizations involved in habitat restoration projects. It could involve planting native species, removing invasive plants, or participating in other initiatives that benefit the ecosystem you explore as a forager.

Many community gardens or local environmental organizations hold volunteer days focused on planting native species or removing invasive plants. Participating in these events is a great way to give back to the natural world, connect with your community, and learn skills for creating a healthy ecosystem.

This chapter has laid the groundwork, equipping you with the foundational knowledge and ethical considerations for responsible and rewarding foraging adventures. However, the true journey begins now. In the following chapters, you'll explore the Northeast's diverse ecosystems, unveiling the unique edible treasures each one harbors.

You'll explore identifying common and cherished wild edibles, from the vibrant spring greens to the hearty fall mushrooms. You'll learn how to harvest these gifts of nature sustainably, ensuring a collection for both you and future generations. Most importantly, you'll transform your foraged finds into culinary delights and craft unforgettable dishes that showcase the incredible flavors of the wild.

Chapter 2: Essential Tools, Equipment, and Safety

The thrill of the hunt and the satisfaction of a successful find are just a few of the joys that await you on your Northeast foraging adventures. However, before you venture out, you must be well-equipped for a successful, safe, and enjoyable experience.

This chapter is your guide to the tools and equipment that will become your mandatory tools on your foraging journeys. You'll explore everything from the essentials to handy extras that elevate your experience. You'll learn proper identification techniques to ensure you're harvesting the right edibles and explore essential precautions to minimize potential risks in the field.

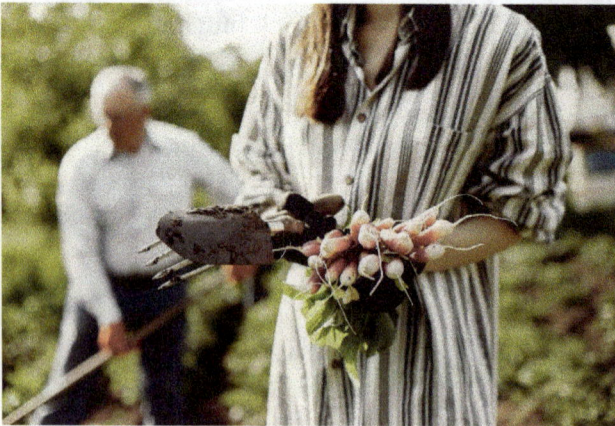

Purchase the needed tools for foraging.[6]

By equipping yourself with the right tools, knowledge, and a healthy dose of caution, you'll be well on your way to transforming your foraging forays into safe, successful, and thoroughly rewarding experiences. Now, grab a seat and prepare for the exciting adventures that lie ahead.

Proper Preparation Practices

The Northeast's wild haul beckons, promising a treasure trove of delicious edibles. However, venturing into the world of foraging requires a commitment to responsible practices and proper preparation. Here's why these aspects are crucial for ensuring safe, successful, and sustainable foraging experiences:

Essential Precautions in the Field

While proper identification is essential, there are additional safety precautions to consider:

- **Be Aware of Your Surroundings:** Pay attention to potential hazards like uneven terrain, poisonous plants (even if you're not foraging them), and wildlife encounters. Let someone know where you're going and when you expect to be back.

- **Dress Appropriately:** Wear sturdy footwear with good ankle support and weather-appropriate clothing, and consider insect repellent depending on the season and location.

- **Know Your Limits:** Don't overexert yourself, especially on unfamiliar terrain. Be mindful of weather changes and plan your foraging trips accordingly.

- **Hydration:** Dehydration sneaks up on you quickly, especially during physical activity in hot weather. Bring plenty of water, and plan to drink regularly throughout your foraging trip. Consider factors like the temperature, humidity, exertion level, and how long you'll be out when determining how much water to pack. In hot or humid conditions, you may need to drink more than you typically would.

- **Sun Protection:** Even on cloudy days, the sun's ultraviolet (UV) rays can damage your skin and eyes. Protect yourself by wearing sunscreen with SPF 30 or higher, a wide-brimmed hat, and sunglasses. Reapply sunscreen every two hours (more often if you're sweating or swimming).

- **Tick and Insect Precautions:** Ticks and insects can carry diseases, so take precautions to avoid them. Wear long pants and long-sleeved shirts treated with insect repellent (permethrin is effective against ticks and mosquitoes). Avoid wearing bright colors that may attract insects. After your foraging trip, do a thorough tick check on yourself and your pets.

- **Tell Someone:** Before heading out on your foraging trip, let a friend or family member know where you're going, the route you plan to take, and when you expect to be back. This way, someone will know if you're overdue and can send help if needed. You can also consider carrying a personal locator beacon (PLB) if you'll be venturing into remote areas without cell service.

Proper preparation is the cornerstone of a successful and enjoyable foraging experience. By prioritizing safe identification, using sustainable harvesting techniques, and taking essential safety precautions, you can explore the Northeast's wilderness with confidence, respect for the environment, and a deep appreciation for the natural world's incredible offerings. Now that you have this information, it's time to learn about the essential tools and equipment that will become your companions on your foraging adventures.

An Introduction to Essential Foraging Tools

You need the right tools before you venture out on your foraging adventures. Here's a closer look at the basic tools you'll need:

The Ultimate Reference

A reliable field guide is your window into the universe of wild edibles. It's your go-to resource for plant identification, offering crucial information to ensure safe and successful foraging:

- **Choose Your Weapon:** Opt for field guides specifically tailored to the Northeastern region. These will provide accurate information on the plants native to your area, ensuring you're not relying on descriptions of look-alikes that might not exist in your local ecosystem.

- **Detailed Descriptions Are Key:** Look for guides with comprehensive descriptions, including high-quality photographs highlighting key identifying features of each plant. These details, such as leaf shape, vein patterns, presence of hairs, and flower color, are crucial for distinguishing safe edibles from their potentially dangerous doppelgangers.

- **Seasonal Variations Matter:** Plants change throughout the year. Invest in a field guide that illustrates plants at various stages of growth, from tender spring shoots to mature flowering forms. This will help you identify your finds accurately, regardless of the season.

Invest in multiple field guides. Refer to Chapter 1 for different resources that offer varied perspectives and additional details that will enhance your identification skills. Consider carrying a pocket-sized guide for quick reference in the field and a more comprehensive guide for in-depth study at home.

Quality Foraging Knife

A sharp, sturdy knife is an essential tool for any forager. It's used for a variety of tasks, ensuring a clean and efficient harvest:

Mushroom foraging knife.[7]

- **Sharpness Is Essential:** Invest in a good quality knife with a sharp blade. A dull blade can damage the plant and make harvesting more difficult. Learn basic knife sharpening techniques to ensure your blade stays sharp and safe to use.

- **The Right Size Matters:** Choose a knife that's comfortable to hold and maneuver in your hand. A smaller knife is ideal for harvesting delicate greens and herbs, while a larger one might be more suitable for cutting through thicker stems or mushrooms.

- **Safety First:** Always practice safe knife handling techniques. Keep your fingers away from the blade, cut on a stable surface, and never carry a loose knife in your pocket.

Consider a folding knife with a locking mechanism for safe and convenient transport. A good option might be a multi-tool that includes a blade, scissors, and a saw, offering additional functionality for various foraging situations. For example, the saw is useful for cutting through tough branches or woody mushrooms.

Sturdy Basket or Foraging Bag

A sturdy basket or foraging bag is essential for carrying your harvested treasures:

Sturdy Basket.⁹

- **Breathable Is Best:** Choose a basket made from natural materials like wicker or straw. These allow for air circulation, preventing your foraged bounty from getting crushed or spoiling. Consider a basket with a ventilated lid for additional protection.

- **Size Matters:** Choose a basket or bag that's comfortable to carry and appropriate for the amount you plan to harvest. A smaller basket might be ideal for quick outings, while a larger bag might be suitable for longer or more fruitful foraging adventures.

- **Consider Multiple Compartments:** A basket or bag with multiple compartments can help you organize your harvest. It's especially useful for separating delicate greens from sturdy mushrooms or keeping different plant species from mingling. Some bags might even have insulated compartments for storing temperature-sensitive items like berries.

Line your basket with a clean cloth or paper towel to help absorb any moisture and prevent your foraged goods from bruising. You can also bring a cooler with ice packs, especially on hot days, to ensure highly perishable items like berries or mushrooms stay fresh during your journey home.

Magnifying Glass or Hand Lens

A magnifying glass or hand lens is a valuable tool for identifying key plant characteristics, especially for beginners:

Magnifying glass.[9]

- **Zooming in on Details:** Certain features like tiny hairs on stems, intricate vein patterns on leaves, or subtle variations in flower structure are crucial for distinguishing between edible and toxic look-alikes. A magnifying glass helps you to examine these details closely and confidently confirm your identification.

- **Compact and Convenient:** Choose a hand lens that's small and lightweight for easy transport in your pocket or foraging bag. Opt for a lens with a magnification power of around 5x to 10x, which is ideal for examining the intricacies of most wild edibles.

- **Double-Duty Tool:** A magnifying glass can also help inspect your harvest for any potential insect visitors or signs of damage before consuming your foraged bounty.

Practical Tip: Consider a magnifying glass with a built-in LED light source. It's beneficial for identifying plants in low light conditions or for examining the often-hidden undersides of leaves where key identification features might reside.

Reusable Cloth Bags and Containers

You can use glass jars to store your foraged goods.[10]

While not essential, incorporating reusable options into your foraging kit demonstrates a commitment to sustainable practices:

- **Reduce, Reuse, Recycle:** Bring reusable cloth bags for larger items or for transporting your harvest home. It minimizes your reliance on single-use plastic bags and contributes to a more eco-friendly foraging experience.

- **Multipurpose Marvels:** Reusable containers are used to store your foraged treasures once you're back home. Opt for breathable containers for delicate greens and airtight containers for mushrooms or berries. Glass jars are another great option for long-term storage of foraged goods.

- **Labeling Is Crucial:** If you're using multiple containers, consider labeling them with the contents and date of harvest. It helps with organization and ensures you remember what you've foraged, especially if you plan to preserve your bounty for later use.

Invest in a reusable water bottle to stay hydrated during your foraging adventures. Not only is it eco-friendly, but it also ensures you have easy access to water throughout your explorations. By equipping yourself with these essential tools and adopting responsible practices, you'll be well on your way to becoming a confident and successful forager.

Cultivating a Risk-Aware Mindset

Venturing out for a successful harvest of wild edibles requires prioritizing your safety above all else. Here's how to cultivate a risk-aware mindset and ensure your foraging experiences are enjoyable, safe, and responsible:

Be Aware of Your Surroundings

Foraging isn't just about identifying plants but being mindful of your environment. Here's how to stay alert to potential hazards:

- **Know Your Limits:** Don't venture out alone, especially if you're new to foraging. Let someone know where you're going and when you expect to be back. Stick to familiar trails and avoid exploring areas with uneven terrain or dense vegetation that could obscure potential dangers.

- **Respect Wildlife:** Wild animals are unpredictable. Be aware of your surroundings and avoid disturbing wildlife habitats. If you encounter an animal, stay calm and back away slowly. Carry bear spray or another form of animal deterrent if you're venturing into areas with a high concentration of large predators.

- Mind the Elements: Check the weather forecast before heading out and dress appropriately. Be prepared for sudden changes in weather conditions. Bring insect repellent, sunscreen, and a hat, depending on the season and location.

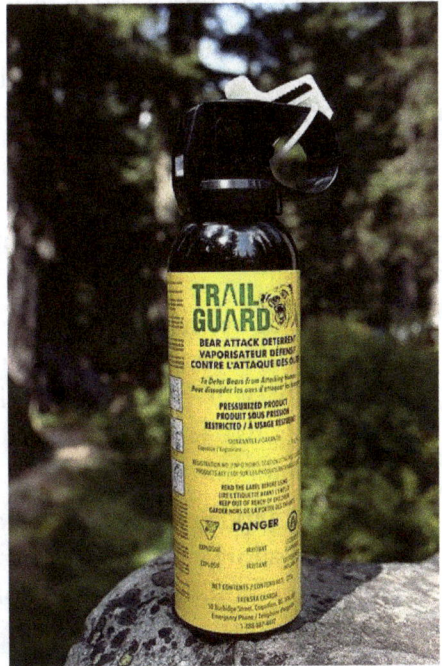

Carry a bear spray with you.[11]

Being aware of your surroundings and potential hazards minimizes the risk of accidents or injuries while exploring. Safety is paramount, so take precautions to ensure you enjoy your foraging adventures to the fullest.

Avoiding Overexertion and Fatigue

Foraging can be an active pursuit, so it's crucial to listen to your body and avoid overexertion:

- **Stay Hydrated:** Carry a reusable water bottle and take regular rehydration breaks, especially on hot days. Dehydration leads to fatigue and impaired judgment and increases the risk of accidents.

- **Pack Light:** Don't overload yourself with unnecessary gear. Only bring what you need. A lightweight backpack is ideal for carrying your essential tools and harvested bounty.

- **Know Your Limits:** Don't push yourself too hard, especially on unfamiliar terrain. Take breaks when needed, and be mindful of potential muscle strain or fatigue.

Listening to your body ensures you enjoy your foraging trip safely and comfortably. Avoiding overexertion minimizes the risk of injuries and allows you to focus on the joy of discovery and the beauty of the natural world around you.

Embrace a Learning Mindset

The world of foraging is a continuous learning journey. Here's how to keep up to date

- **Attend Workshops or Courses:** Consider attending workshops or online courses led by experienced foragers. These resources will teach you proper identification techniques, safe harvesting methods, and additional safety precautions specific to your region.

- **Stay Updated on Regulations:** Be aware of any local or state regulations regarding foraging in your area. These regulations might limit the harvesting of particular species or restrict foraging in specific protected areas.

- **Connect with a Foraging Community:** Join online forums or local foraging groups to connect with other enthusiasts. These communities are a valuable source of information and are a platform to share your experiences and learn from others.

Continuously educating yourself and staying informed minimizes risks and ensures your foraging practices are safe, responsible, and respectful of the environment. Venturing into the Northeast requires a commitment to responsible practices and a deep respect for nature's power and its potential hazards. With the proper knowledge, preparation, and a safety-first approach, you will confidently forage wild edibles.

Potential Hazards and Safe Foraging Practices

The Northeast's wild landscapes are a treasure trove of edible delights. However, you have to be aware of potential hazards. Understanding these challenges and adopting safe practices will make your foraging adventures rewarding and risk-free. Here's a closer look at some common dangers and how to navigate them with confidence:

Poisonous Plants

The most significant danger is undoubtedly poisonous plants. Here's how to minimize the risk of mistaken identity:

- **Positive Identification Is Key:** There's no substitute for proper plant identification. Always consult reliable field guides and online resources from reputable institutions, and if possible, seek confirmation from an experienced forager before consuming any wild plant.

- **Beware of Look-Alikes:** Many edible plants have poisonous doppelgangers that are deceptively similar. Learn to recognize the subtle differences distinguishing safe edibles from their dangerous counterparts. Focus on multiple identifying features, such as leaf shape, vein patterns, flower color, and hairiness on stems, and never rely on a single characteristic for confirmation.

- **When in Doubt, Leave It Out:** This golden rule applies whenever you're unsure about a plant's identity. Err on the side of caution and leave it where it is. It's always better to be safe than sorry.

Additional Tips

- **Learn Plant Families:** Familiarize yourself with the characteristics of common plant families in your region. It'll help you narrow down the possibilities when encountering an unknown plant.

- **Start with Easy-to-Identify Species:** As a beginner, focus on foraging for well-known and easily identifiable edibles before venturing into more challenging territory.

Uneven Ground, Slippery Surfaces, and Hidden Hazards

The beauty of the Northeast wilderness sometimes masks hidden dangers. Here's how to stay safe on uneven terrain:

- **Stick to Designated Trails:** Whenever possible, stay on well-maintained trails. These paths are less likely to have hidden hazards like loose rocks, uneven ground, or drop-offs.

- **Mind Your Footing:** Pay attention to where you step, especially on uneven terrain or in areas with loose soil or rocks. Wear sturdy footwear with good ankle support for better traction and stability.

- **Be Aware of Your Surroundings:** Don't get so engrossed in searching for plants that you neglect your surroundings. Watch out for hidden holes, fallen trees, or slippery surfaces, especially after rain or snowfall.

Additional Tips

- **Use Trekking Poles:** Consider using trekking poles for added stability, especially on uneven ground.

- **Plan Your Route:** Before heading out, research the area you plan to explore and be aware of any potential hazards like steep inclines, loose rocks, or bodies of water.

- **Let Someone Know Your Plans:** Inform a friend or family member about your intended route and estimated return time. This ensures someone can raise the alarm if you don't return as planned.

Use trekking poles for stability on uneven ground.[12]

Unpredictable Wildlife

The Northeast is home to a variety of wildlife, some of which can pose a threat if startled or approached too closely. Here's how to minimize the risk of wildlife encounters:

- **Be Aware of Your Surroundings:** Pay attention to animal sounds and signs like tracks or droppings. It'll help you identify areas with a higher concentration of wildlife and avoid disturbing them.

- **Make Noise:** Make noise as you walk, especially in areas with dense vegetation where animals might be hidden. It alerts them to your presence, and you'll avoid a surprise encounter.

- **Keep a Safe Distance:** If you encounter wildlife, maintain a safe distance and avoid approaching them. Never attempt to feed or corner a wild animal.

Additional Tips

- **Carry Bear Spray (If Applicable):** In areas with a high concentration of large predators like bears, carrying bear spray is a good idea, as is knowing how to use it safely and legally.

- **Research Local Wildlife:** Before venturing into a new area, research the types of wildlife you might encounter and familiarize yourself with their behavior.

- **Dress Appropriately:** Avoid wearing bright colors or strong scents, which can attract some wildlife. Opt for neutral-colored clothing that blends in with the natural environment.

Understanding these potential dangers and foraging safely will minimize risks and ensure your explorations are enjoyable and responsible.

Tips on Maintaining and Caring for Your Foraging Tools

Your foraging tools are your trusted companions on your wild, edible adventures. Like any valuable equipment, proper care and maintenance are necessary to ensure their longevity and effectiveness. Here are some tips to keep your gear in top condition:

A Sharp Blade Is a Safe Blade

A sharp knife is vital for clean cuts.

- **Invest in a Quality Sharpener:** Opt for a good quality whetstone or honing steel specifically designed for sharpening knives. Avoid using generic kitchen sharpeners that damage the blade.

- **Learn Proper Sharpening Techniques:** Different sharpening techniques exist for various knife types. Take the time to learn the proper method for your specific knife to ensure you're sharpening it effectively. Consider attending a knife sharpening workshop or watching instructional videos online.

- **Regular Sharpening Is Key:** Don't wait for your knife to become dull before sharpening it. Regular honing sessions keep the edge sharp and prevent the blade from becoming damaged. A good rule of thumb is honing your knife after a few foraging trips or extensive use.

Practical Tip: After each use, especially after cutting through tough materials, clean your knife with a damp cloth and dry it thoroughly before storing it. It prevents rust and ensures your blade stays sharp for longer.

Keeping Your Basket or Foraging Bag Clean and Functional

Your basket or bag plays a crucial role in transporting your foraged treasures. Here's how to maintain its functionality and lifespan:

- **Empty and Air It Out:** After each foraging trip, empty your basket or bag. Brush or wipe away any dirt, debris, or leftover plant material. Allow it to air out thoroughly before storing it to prevent moisture buildup and potential mold growth.

- **Spot Cleaning for Minor Stains:** For minor stains, use a damp cloth with a gentle cleaning solution (like a mild soap and water mixture) to wipe down the affected areas. Allow them to dry completely before storing.

- **Deep Cleaning for Stubborn Stains:** For tougher stains or persistent dirt, consider a more thorough cleaning depending on the material of your basket or bag. Some natural fiber baskets might benefit from a light brushing with a soft brush, while canvas bags might be hand-washable according to the manufacturer's instructions.

Practical Tip: Invest in a basket liner made from breathable fabric. It'll catch any dirt or debris, making cleaning your basket even easier. Additionally, the liner can be washed separately, keeping your basket looking fresh for longer.

Caring for Your Magnifying Glass or Hand Lens

A magnifying glass or hand lens helps you see the intricate details of plants for accurate identification. Here's how to keep your lens clear and functional:

- **Lens Cleaning Wipes Are Your Friend:** Invest in lens cleaning wipes specifically designed for optics. Avoid using harsh chemicals, paper towels, or tissues, as these can scratch the delicate lens surface.
- **Dust Matters:** Use a soft brush to gently remove any dust particles from the lens before each use. It ensures a clear view and prevents scratches.
- **Store It Safely:** When not in use, store your magnifying glass or hand lens in a protective case to prevent accidental damage from scratches or crushing.

Consider attaching your magnifying glass or hand lens to your basket or foraging bag with a secure clip or carabiner. It keeps it readily accessible and minimizes the risk of losing it during your explorations.

Sustainable Solutions for Long-Term Use

Reusable cloth bags and containers are eco-friendly alternatives for transporting and storing your foraged bounty. Here's how to keep them in good condition:

- **Washing Is Essential:** Wash your reusable cloth bags and containers after each use. Follow the manufacturer's instructions for washing, which might involve handwashing or using a gentle cycle on your washing machine.
- **Air Drying Is Best:** Air-dry your reusable bags and containers whenever possible instead of using a machine dryer. The high heat from a dryer damages some materials and shortens their lifespan.
- **Inspect for Damage:** Regularly inspect your reusable bags and containers for signs of wear and tear, such as rips, tears, or loose stitching. Repair any minor damage promptly to prevent further deterioration.

Addressing Minor Repairs

Minor repairs addressed promptly significantly extend the lifespan of your foraging gear. Here's how to stay ahead of potential problems:

- **Be Proactive:** Regularly inspect your basket, bags, and straps for any signs of wear and tear, such as loose stitching, fraying edges, or broken zippers.

- **DIY Repairs Are Doable:** Consider a DIY fix for minor repairs like loose stitching or a ripped seam. Numerous online tutorials and resources exist to guide you through simple repairs for materials like canvas, wicker, or nylon.

- **Seek Professional Help for Major Issues:** For more complex repairs beyond your skillset, take your gear to a professional cobbler, tailor, or leatherworker for repairs. Their expertise can ensure your favorite foraging companions are restored to functionality for many more adventures.

Practical Tip: Invest in a basic sewing kit containing needles, thread, and scissors. It allows you to address minor repairs like loose stitching or a popped button on the spot, keeping your gear functional and extending its lifespan.

These simple tips and maintaining your foraging tools ensure they're reliable companions but also safe and effective for countless future foraging adventures.

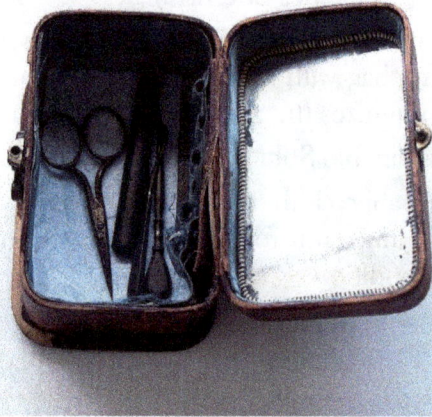

Invest in a sewing kit.[18]

Taking care of your gear shows respect for your investment and allows you to focus on the true joy of exploring the world of wild edibles.

The right tools will elevate your experience. A reliable field guide becomes your window into the types of wild edibles, while a sharp knife ensures clean cuts and promotes safety. A sturdy basket or bag allows you to carry your bounty with pride, while a magnifying glass helps you uncover the intricate details of plants for accurate identification. The most valuable tool a forager possesses is a keen sense of observation. The ability to identify plants, recognize potential dangers, and respect the ecosystem's delicate balance is what truly sets you apart.

Chapter 3: Seasonal Foraging in the Northeast

The Northeast's wild landscapes are woven with dynamic colors and ever-changing textures. Spring bursts forth with tender greens, summer explodes in a riot of color and fragrant blooms, autumn paints the scene in fiery hues, and winter cloaks the land in a serene blanket of white. Apart from being visually captivating, this dynamic landscape offers a unique bounty that transforms with each passing season.

The Northeast's wild landscapes are woven with dynamic colors and ever-changing textures.[14]

In this chapter, you'll peel back the layers of this captivating experience. You'll discover how the changing seasons dictate the availability of wild edibles, transforming each foraging adventure into a unique and ever-evolving treasure hunt. From the delicate shoots of spring to the earthly delights of autumn and the unexpected finds of winter, you'll be able to explore the diverse palette of flavors and textures the Northeast offers throughout the year.

This chapter is about identifying and harvesting a variety of seasonal delicacies. You'll learn about the ideal times to search for specific plants, discover expert tips on sustainable harvesting techniques, and learn how to preserve your bounty for future enjoyment. Prepare to unlock the secrets of the seasons, one foraged treasure at a time.

Spring: A Season of Renewal and Awakened Flavors

Spring in the Northeast is a time of vibrant awakening. As the winter's icy grip loosens and the earth thaws, a surge of life pushes forth, painting the landscape with a palette of tender greens and delicate blooms. This season marks the beginning of a delicious adventure for foragers, offering a bounty of fresh, young growth bursting with flavor and essential nutrients after a long winter. Following is a deep dive into the delights that usually emerge during this time!

The First Edible Shoots and Greens (March-April)

As the snow melts and the first rays of warm sunshine kiss the earth, a select group of early risers emerge. These pioneering plants pave the way for the abundance of summer, offering a taste of the season's potential.

Edible fiddleheads of the ostrich fern (*Matteuccia struthiopteris*).[15]

- **Fiddleheads:** Unfurl your taste buds for fiddleheads, the tightly coiled fronds of ferns. These emerald wonders are a Northeast springtime delicacy with a unique fiddle-like shape that makes them easily identifiable. Not all ferns produce edible fiddleheads, however, so consult a field guide before harvesting and always harvest in moderation.

Morel Mushroom (*Morchella* spp.).[16]

- **Morel Mushrooms:** These elusive mushrooms, with their hollow stems and chambered caps, are prized for their meaty texture and earthy flavor. However, watch out for toxic lookalikes, which can superficially resemble true morels. Always consult with an expert mycologist or forager before eating any wild mushroom for the first time.

Ramps (*Allium tricoccum*).[17]

- **Ramps:** Often called wild leeks – and closely related to both garlic (*A. sativum*) and wild onions (*A. canadense*) – ramps add a delightful garlicky kick to spring dishes. Look for their broad, flat leaves, which usually wither before the distinctive white flowers unfurl. Ramps are a versatile ingredient, perfect for adding depth of flavor to soups, pastas, and even pestos.

Fun Fact: Did you know that fiddleheads hold a special place in some cultures? In Japan, certain fiddleheads are called "*warabi*" (bracken fern) and are considered a prized ingredient in traditional cuisine? They are frequently served whole as a refreshing appetizer, and the starch they contain is used to make a jelly-like cake called *warabi-mochi* ("warabi cake").

Tender Leaves and Emerging Herbs (April-May)

As spring progresses, the landscape explodes with a vibrant tapestry of tender greens. This is the time to celebrate the return of fresh herbs and leafy vegetables, offering a welcome change from the root vegetables that dominated winter menus.

- **Dandelions (_Taraxacum_ spp.):** Don't underestimate the humble dandelion. Every part of this plant is edible, from the bright yellow flowers to the distinctive leaves. The young leaves have a slightly bitter flavor that is perfect for adding a peppery kick to salads or stir-fries, while the older leaves can be cooked much like mustard greens or kale. Dandelion flowers can be used to make fritters or even transformed into a vibrant yellow wine.

Flowers and bulblets of wild garlic (*Allium canadense*).[18]

- **Wild Garlic:** Closely related to the ramps, wild garlic emerges a bit later in spring. The bulbs, greens and bulblets (small bulbs produced in place of flowers) are edible and delicious, with a distinctive scent and flavor similar to garlic. The greens can be used in place of cultivated garlic, adding a delightful bite to pestos and soups, while the whole plants can be used like leeks or green onions – they are especially delicious grilled.

Young stinging nettle (*Urtica dioica*) plants.[19]

- **Nettles:** Nettles might seem like a foe at first glance (or touch) due to the painful stining hairs that cover their stems and leaves. However, once these are removed – either by cooking or soaking -- they transform into a delicious and nutritious green. Packed with vitamins and minerals, nettles offer a mild, spinach-like flavor that complements various dishes. Harvest the youngest leaves, and only from plants that haven't flowered yet, as older plants become tough and stringy – and remember to wear gloves!

Fun Fact: Dandelions are more than just a common lawn weed. Their greens are a nutritional powerhouse, boasting a wealth of vitamins, minerals, and antioxidants, and both roots and leaves have been used in herbal medicine for millennia.

Early Berries and Spring Flowers (May-June)

Spring isn't just about savory delights. This season also unveils a treasure trove of sweet surprises in the form of early-blooming berries and edible flowers.

Wild strawberry (*Fragaria vesca*) flower and fruits.[20]

- **Wild Strawberries:** Forget the supermarket giants and keep an eye out for wild strawberries. These tiny gems, bursting with concentrated flavor, are a hidden treasure often overlooked in favor of their cultivated cousins. Look for them in sunny woodland edges and clearings in early summer, and enjoy their intense sweetness fresh or in jams and desserts

- **Elder:** Common in sunny, disturbed soils, especially near water, both the flowers and fruits of the black elder (*Sambucus nigra*) are edible: the flowers have a light, floral aroma that elevates syrups, jams, and even cocktails, while the berries are tart, sweet, and earthy. Keep in mind that both flowers and fruits should be cooked thoroughly before consumption, as they can be toxic when eaten raw. Look for the conspicuous flat-topped white flower clusters along fencerows, roadsides, and river banks.

- **Violets:** Violets (*Viola* spp.) are not just symbols of spring – their leaves and flowers are edible and delicious. The delicate blooms can be candied, made into tea, or tossed into salads for a pop of color, while the young leaves have a mild, green flavor perfect for salads or garnishes.

Fun Fact: Elder has been used for centuries in traditional medicine for its purported health benefits, and remains one of the most widely used medicinal plants in the world. The fragrant elderflower cordial, a syrup made from the blossoms, is a popular drink in many European countries and is believed to have soothing properties for coughs and colds.

Spring is an invitation to witness the landscape's transformation and capitalize on the vibrancy and freshness of the season's offerings. With a keen eye and a basket in hand, you'll undertake a delightful journey of discovery, savoring the unique flavors that herald the arrival of spring in the Northeast.

Summer's Feast for the Senses

Spring's vibrant awakening gives way to summer's exuberant explosion. Lush green landscapes become a dazzling display of wildflowers while trees groan under the weight of ripening fruits and nuts. This season marks the peak of nature's bounty in the Northeast, offering a smorgasbord of delicious edibles for the discerning forager. Here's a glimpse into the diverse offerings summer has in store:

Wild Fruits Take Center Stage (June-August)

Summer paints the Northeast with a vibrant palette of juicy, sweet, and tart wild fruits. From the delicate sweetness of raspberries to the tangy allure of wild blueberries, these edible gems offer a refreshing and flavorful reward for your foraging efforts.

- **Berry Bonanza:** In summer, berries of all kinds transform the landscape into a forager's paradise: raspberries and blackberries, (*Rubus* spp.), blueberries and huckleberries (*Vaccinium* spp.), and currants and gooseberries (*Ribes* spp.), to name just a few. These juicy delights can be enjoyed fresh off the bush, used to make jams, pies, and cobblers, or even frozen for later enjoyment. Harvest berries at their peak ripeness for the best flavor and nutritional value. To ensure a sustainable harvest, focus on picking only a few of the ripest berries from a single plant, and leaving plenty behind for the wildlife and regeneration.

- **Hidden Gems:** Don't overlook lesser-known wild fruits like elderberries and chokecherries (*Prunus virginiana*). Elderberries, with their deep purple clusters, can be used to make syrups, jams, and even jellies, while chokecherries, once processed to moderate their natural bitterness, can be transformed into delicious jams, pies, and even wines. Don't neglect these under-appreciated fruits: they make a unique and flavorful addition to your summer repertoire.

Fun Fact: Did you know that raspberries, blackberries, dewberries, and other brambles (*Rubus* spp.) aren't berries? They aren't even individual fruits: instead, they are classified as "aggregate fruits," meaning they develop from a single flower with multiple ovaries. Each tiny "pip" you see on a raspberry is a separate fruit, called a *druplelet*, which cluster together to form the juicy treat you know and love. Only plants in the genus *Rubus* produce these distinctive fruits, and all are safe to eat, making them an excellent place to start for beginning foragers.

Savory Additions for Your Summer Table (June-August)

Summer's bounty isn't just about sweet treats. This season also offers a diverse array of edible greens that can add a touch of freshness and unique flavors to your summer dishes.

- **Salad Sensations:** Purslane (*Portulaca oleracea*), a succulent annual often encountered as a weed in gardens and sidewalks, is a nutritional powerhouse: rich in vitamins and minerals, it's also high in omega-3 fatty acids like those found in salmon and chia seeds. It has a slightly sour flavor that adds a delightful twist to summer salads. Goosefoot (*Chenopodium album*), also called wild spinach and lamb's quarters, is equally nutritious (the greens are exceptionally high in protein) and equally versatile: perfect for salads, stir-fries, or served alone as a delicious side dish. When harvesting greens, be mindful of the plant's overall health: take only a few leaves from each plant, leaving most of the plant behind to ensure its continued growth (and a sustainable harvest all season long).

- **Foraging for Flavor:** Explore the world of wild herbs like garlic, ramps, and wood sorrel (*Oxalis* spp.). Ramps add depth to summer dishes with their intense garlic flavor, while wood sorrel enlivens salads and sauces with its lemony tang. Snip only the top leaves and newer growth when foraging for herbs, allowing the plant to continue producing throughout the season.

Fun Fact: Purslane is one of the most resilient plants on the planet. It thrives in hot, dry conditions and can often be found growing happily from cracks in roads and sidewalks. This tenacity makes it a valuable addition to any forager's repertoire, as it's often readily available when most other greens are either wilting or becoming unpalatably tough .

Nuts Ripen and Mushrooms Emerge (July-August)

While summer's peak sweetness reigns, nature also offers a glimpse into the bounty of fall. This is when some early-maturing nuts begin to ripen, and the first mushrooms start peeking through the forest floor.

- **Early Nut Treasures:** With a sweet and nutty flavor similar to common European hazelnuts (*Corylus avelllana*), native hazelnuts (*C. americana*) are some of the first nuts to ripen in the Northeast. Look for these low, slender shrubs nestled in the understory of old-growth forests. The distinctive catkins (long strands of tiny flowers) emerge in early spring, which mature into nuts over the summer. The nuts are enclosed in odd-looking leafy bracts, which begin to brown and split when the nuts are ready to harvest.

- **Mushroom Mania:** For the experienced mushroom forager, summer offers a chance to hunt for chanterelles (*Cantharellus* spp.) and hen-of-the-woods (*Grifola frondosa*) mushrooms. These prized edibles add meaty texture and complex, earthy flavors to summer dishes. However, proper identification is crucial, as mushrooms are challenging to identify by appearance alone, and among the edibles are many toxic look-alikes. Consult a reliable mushroom guide, and always forage with experienced individuals: not only is it safer, burt even if you come home empty-handed, you'll have enjoyed good company and conversation.

Fun Fact: Did you know that hazelnuts are not really nuts? They are classified as "drupes," like peaches or almonds (no, almonds aren't nuts either!) . While the hard, edible kernel resembles a true nut, it's surrounded by a fleshy husk, a defining characteristic of drupes. Whatever you call them, hazelnuts remain a delicious and nutritious addition to any forager's summer harvest.

By understanding summer's diverse offerings and employing responsible harvesting techniques, you can make the most of this season's abundance. Summer is a forager's dream, from the juicy sweetness of berries to the savory delights of wild greens and the promise of early nuts and mushrooms.

Autumn's Abundance

Summer's greens give way to a captivating spectacle as fall paints the Northeast landscape in a fiery tapestry of oranges, reds, and yellows. The air turns crisp, and the once-lush foliage transforms into a breathtaking display of color. However, for foragers, autumn is more than just a visual feast.

Nature's Fall Feast (September-October)

As the leaves begin to fall, a treasure trove of nuts ripens on the branches of trees throughout the Northeast. These crunchy delights offer a satisfying and nutritious reward for the patient forager.

- **Acorns Aplenty:** Acorns from oak trees (*Quercus* spp.) are perhaps the quintessential symbol of fall – and it may surprise you to learn that you can eat them, too! However, not all acorns are created equal: most oaks contain significant ammounts of tannins, extremely bitter compounds that must be leached (either by boiling in several changes of water or soaking for several days) before consumption. Some species, like the common white oak *(Q. alba)* and swamp white oak *(Q. bicolor)*, have relatively sweet, low-tannin acorns, which are perfect for roasting like chestnuts, boiling like peanuts, or even grinding into flour. When harvesting acorns, make sure to avoid acorns with cracked shells, discolored kernels, or holes (made by worms). If you can find them, look for recently sprouted acorns: they are not only guaranteed to be free of worms and other parasites,, but they are sweeter than newly fallen acorns.

Beechnut.[21]

- **Beechnut Bonanza:** Beech trees (*Fagus* spp.) have triangular "nuts" with a sweet and slightly bitter or earthy flavor. Enjoy them raw, roasted, or ground into flour for a unique addition to your fall baking. Harvest beechnuts when the brown husks split open, indicating they're ripe and ready to fall. Sustainable harvesting practices are especially important for beechnuts, as they are a valuable food source for deer, bears, and other mammals preparing for winter.

- **Hickory Treasures:** Hickory nuts (*Carya* spp.), encased in tough husks, can be a challenge to crack but are well worth the effort. Their rich, buttery flavor makes them a prized ingredient in fall dishes and desserts. Pro tip: rather than struggle with the husks, just leave the nuts in the sun for a few days. As the husks dry out, they'll naturally split open.

Fun Fact: Did you know that squirrels aren't the only ones who enjoy acorns? Certain species of woodpeckers, bluejays, and deer are just a few of the animals that rely on acorns as a winter food source. By practicing sustainable harvesting, you're ensuring a bountiful harvest not just for yourself, but for the wildlife that calls the Northeast home.

Seeds of Change (September-October)

Fall isn't just about harvesting the bounty of the present season. It's also about preparing for the future. Wild seeds, scattered by nature, offer a glimpse into next spring's potential and a chance to cultivate your own foraged food source.

Milkweed.[22]

- **Milkweed Marvels:** Look for distinctive milkweed (*Asclepias* spp.) pods bursting with feathery seeds. Once the pods dry and split open, the seeds can be collected and saved for future planting. Milkweed is a vital host plant for the caterpillars of the endangered monarch butterfly (*Danaus plexippus*), so consider planting some to create a haven for these beautiful pollinators. By planting milkweed (and other pollinator-friendly plants), you can contribute to the conservation of native pollinators and the services they provide humans.

Sunflower.[38]

- Sunflower Surprises: Don't overlook the brown, wrinkled heads of wild sunflowers (*Helianthus* spp.). These are likely to contain an abundance of small black seeds, perfect for attracting birds to your backyard or for planting in the spring for next year. Planting wildflower seeds, like those from sunflowers, not only provides a winter food source for birds but also helps beautify your landscape and create a haven for pollinators.

- **Wild Cruciferous Riches:** Keep an eye out for the bean-like seed pods (or *siliques*) of plants in the cabbage family (Brassicaceae) like black

Wild Arugula.[34]

mustard (*Brassica nigra*), wild arugula (*Diplotaxis tenuifolia*), and others. These can be collected and used as a spice, or stored for planting later – ensuring a fresh supply of this delightful salad green next spring. Foraging for seeds expands your repertoire beyond just the current season's offerings. By planting these wild seeds, you become a steward of the natural world, promoting biodiversity and ensuring the continuation of these plants.

Fun Fact: Wild seeds are nature's way of ensuring the survival of plant species. By scattering them in the wind, on the water, or through the actions of animals, these seeds find new homes and spread the plant's territory. By collecting and planting wild seeds, you become a partner in this natural cycle, fostering biodiversity and promoting the growth of native plants.

The Last of the Summer Fruits (September-October)

While summer's peak berry season might be over, fall offers a delightful surprise in the form of late-ripening berries that add a touch of sweetness to the changing landscape.

- **Cranberry Delights:**

  Cranberries (*Vaccinium* spp.), with their vibrant red hue and tart flavor, are a quintessential symbol of autumn. Look for them in low-lying marshy areas, especially on acidic soils. Wear waterproof boots, as the terrain they occur on is often quite mucky. Sustainable harvesting is crucial for cranberries, so pick only ripe berries.

- **Mountain Ash Majesty:**

  The vibrant orange berries of the mountain ash (*Sorbus aucuparia*), which ripen in autumn, are quite bitter even

Cranberry (*Vaccinium macrocarpon*).[25]

when ripe – but they can be transformed into delicious jellies and jams once properly processed. When harvesting mountain ash berries, wait until after the first frost, as freezing this mellows their bitterness. Keep in mind that many red fruits are toxic, and always consult a reliable guide before consuming wild berries.

Mountain ash (*Sorbus aucuparia*).[26]

- **Elderberry Encore:** Elderberries, with their deep purple clusters, offer a second chance for foragers in the fall. While spring elderflowers are prized for their fragrant syrups, the fall berries can be used to make jams, jellies, and even wines. Cook elderberries thoroughly before eating, as raw berries can be mildly toxic. Sustainable harvesting is also key for elderberries, so pick only ripe berries and leave plenty on the branches for birds and other wildlife.

Fun Fact: Did you know that cranberries can bounce? These unique berries contain air pockets that allow them to float and be easily dispersed by water. This adaptation helps cranberries travel long distances, establishing new colonies in suitable wetland habitats.

As fall unfolds, the Northeast landscape transforms into a vibrant tapestry of colors, offering a seasonal fall crop for the discerning forager. From the satisfying crunch of nuts to the unexpected sweetness of late-season berries, autumn presents a chance to savor the last whispers of summer and prepare for the winter slumber to come. Responsible and sustainable harvesting ensures there's enough for everyone, humans and wildlife alike. So, embrace the crisp autumn air, explore the changing landscapes, and enjoy the final chapter of nature's Northeast bounty before winter arrives.

Winter's Hidden Treasures: A Forager's Unexpected Delights

As the first snowflakes fall and the Northeast landscape cloaks itself in white, you might assume the season for foraging is over. However, winter unveils a surprising array of hidden treasures for the keen observer. While the abundance of summer and fall may be absent, winter offers an opportunity to discover the resilience of certain other plants and fungi, rewarding patient foragers with unexpected delights.

Plants That Thrive in the Cold (December-February)

While much of the plant world retreats during winter, some resilient species remain green and vibrant, offering a welcome surprise for the forager who knows where to look.

Rosemary (*Salvia rosmarinus*).[27]

- **Evergreen Herbs:** Rosemary (*Salvia rosmarinus*), thyme (*Thymus pulegoides*), and other evergreen herbs defy the winter chill, keeping their fragrance and flavor throughout the colder months. These culinary staples can be used fresh or dried to add a special touch to your dishes. Pick only what you need, allowing the plant to thrive through the harsh winter.

- **Ferns and Their Kin:** Certain fern varieties, like Christmas fern (Polystichum acrosticoides) and maidenhair fern *(Adiantum pedatum)*, retain their verdant beauty throughout winter. While not edible, they can still add a touch of spring's green to winter bouquets and centerpieces, reminding you of nature's enduring spirit.

- **Roots and Shoots:** Some plants store energy below the frozen soil in the form of edible roots, tubers, and dormant shoots. With proper identification and responsible practices, you can unearth treasures like burdock root (*Arctium lappa*) or sunchokes (*Helianthus tuberosus*) and enjoy them in winter stews and soups.

Fun Fact: Did you know that some plants benefit from a cold spell? Some plants require vernalization, or exposure to cold winter temperatures, in order to flower and produce fruit in the spring. While the winter landscape might seem barren, beneath the surface, nature is quietly working its magic, preparing for the explosion of life to come.

The Hunt for Winter Mushrooms (December-February)

For the experienced forager, winter offers a thrilling challenge of the hunt for winter mushrooms. While mushroom foraging requires extreme caution and proper identification skills, some varieties thrive under a light snow cover, waiting to be discovered by the adventurous gatherer.

- **Oyster Mushrooms:** With their distinctive fan-shaped caps and creamy white or gray coloring, oyster mushrooms (*Pleurotus ostreatus*) can often be found clustered on logs or dead trees throughout the winter, especially in early winter or spring after a cold snap. Consult a reliable mushroom guide and never ingest any wild mushroom without absolute certainty of its identification.

Oyster mushrooms (*Pleurotus ostreatus*).[28]

- **Lion's Mane:** With its cascading, icicle-like spines, lion's mane (*Hericium* spp.) adds texture and flavor to winter dishes. Lion's mane mushrooms are also distinctive, with no toxic lookalikes, making them good species for beginners – but remember, *always* consult an experienced forager or mycologist before eating a wild mushroom.

Bear's head tooth (*Hericium americanum*), a species of lion's mane mushroom.[29]

- **Hen-of-the-Woods:** Don't be fooled by the snow. Hen-of-the-woods mushrooms (*Grifola frondosa*), prized for their meaty texture and earthy flavor, can sometimes be found at the base of trees even during the coldest months. Prioritize safety above all else, and only eat wild mushrooms after checking with a reliable guide.

Hen-of-the-woods (*Grifola frondosa*)[30]

Season	Forageables	Foraging Tips
Spring	Fiddleheads, Ramps, Wild greens, Early berries	Focus on young, tender growth for the best flavor. Only harvest a small portion of what you find to ensure sustainability. Learn to properly identify each plant before consuming. Consult a local foraging guide or expert for specific location tips.
Summer	Berries, Nuts, Edible flowers, Wild greens	Look for ripe berries with vibrant colors. Avoid picking nuts from the ground, as they might be rotten. Choose edible flowers that haven't bloomed fully yet. Harvest wild greens during cooler mornings for better texture.
Autumn	Nuts, Seeds, Late-season berries	Wear gloves when harvesting nuts to protect yourself from thorns or spiky shells. Let seeds dry completely before storing them for long-term use. Focus on late-season berries that haven't been overtaken by birds. Research proper drying or storage methods for your harvest.

Season	Forageables	Foraging Tips
Winter	Evergreen herbs, Winter mushrooms (exercise extreme caution and proper identification), Edible roots and shoots	Harvest sparingly from evergreen herbs as growth is slow in winter. Only forage for mushrooms with a trusted guide or expert to avoid poisonous lookalikes. Dig for edible roots and shoots carefully, avoiding damaging surrounding plants. Be aware of freezing temperatures and plan your foraging trips accordingly.

Fun Fact: Did you know that some winter mushrooms can help break down dead wood and fallen leaves, returning nutrients to the forest floor? These "decomposers" play a vital role in the forest ecosystem, ensuring the health and continued growth of the trees and plants that depend on them. By understanding the role of winter mushrooms, you gain a deeper appreciation for the interconnectedness of the natural world.

A Seasonal Foraging Calendar

Winter might be the quiet season for foraging, but it's the perfect time to plan your future adventures. By creating a seasonal calendar, you'll chart a year filled with delicious discoveries. **See the Bonus Section for a sample foraging calendar.**

With each season comes a new chapter in the story of the Northeast's wild crop. Spring's vibrant awakening is tender greens and fleeting delights. Summer explodes with a riot of colors and flavors, from juicy berries to the first signs of fall's harvest. Autumn paints the landscape in fiery hues and presents a bounty of nuts, seeds, and late-season berries. Winter, often overlooked, unveils the hidden treasures of resilient plants beneath the snow's cover.

By understanding the resilience of certain plants and winter mushrooms (with utmost caution), you'll extend your foraging adventures throughout the year. Responsible and sustainable harvesting practices are essential during every season. Respect the natural balance, take only what you need, and leave plenty behind for the wildlife and future harvests.

Fun Fact: Did you know that some plants have specific adaptations to survive harsh winter conditions? Evergreen herbs, for example, have a waxy coating on their leaves that helps prevent water loss during freezing temperatures. By understanding these adaptations, you get a deeper appreciation for the resilience of the natural world and the fascinating strategies plants employ to thrive throughout the year.

Chapter 4: Common Wild Edible Plants of the Northeast

Have you ever wandered through the Northeast's landscapes, wondering what lies hidden amongst the verdant greens and colorful wildflowers? The truth is, the wild world around you is teeming with delicious and nutritious edibles. In this chapter, you'll unlock the secrets of nature's pantry, introducing yourself to a selection of the most common wild edible plants that grace the Northeast region.

It's time to explore the fascinating common wild edible plants in the Northeast.[81]

This informative guide focuses on easily recognizable and safe-to-consume plants, helping you to undertake your foraging adventures confidently. From the delicate shoots of spring to the rich berries of summer and the hearty nuts of fall, you'll explore a diverse array of edible delights. Whether you're a seasoned forager seeking to expand your repertoire or a curious newcomer eager to explore wild edibles, this chapter is your essential companion.

So, grab your basket, sharpen your senses, and prepare to be amazed by the abundance that nature offers right under your feet. It's time to explore the fascinating common wild edible plants in the Northeast, where every turn reveals a new potential ingredient waiting to be discovered and enjoyed.

Profiles of Staple Greens

The Northeast is rich in a diverse range of wild greens that add a delightful touch of freshness and unique flavors to your meals. These readily available and easy-to-identify plants are perfect for novice foragers, offering a delicious introduction to wild edibles. It's time to explore three staple greens: the ubiquitous dandelion, the versatile lamb's quarters, and the delicate chickweed.

Dandelion (*Taraxacum officinale*)

The dandelion is a familiar sight throughout the Northeast. Often considered a pesky weed, this tenacious plant offers a bounty of edible treasures, from its bright yellow flowers to its deeply lobed leaves.

The dandelion.[39]

- **Distinct Characteristics:** Dandelions are easily recognizable by their bright yellow composite flowers that transform into fluffy white seed heads. The leaves are deeply lobed with jagged edges, emerging in a rosette at the base of the plant.

- **Preferred Habitats:** Dandelions thrive disturbed soils, and grow abundantly in lawns, gardens, roadsides, and wastelands. Their resilience allows them to flourish even in compacted soils, making them ubiquitous in many urban and suburban landscapes.

- **Seasonal Nuances:** Dandelions grow almost year-round, but grow most abundantly in spring. The greens are best when young, especially before the flower buds appear. The bitter flavor of the leaves increases in flowering plants to protect them from herbivory. Dandelion flowers can be harvested at any time of year for use in wines, jellies, or as a colorful garnish.

- **Nutritional Benefits:** Dandelion greens are a nutritional powerhouse, boasting a rich source of vitamins A, C, and K, as well as potassium and iron. They also contain a unique compound called taraxacin, which is believed to offer liver-detoxifying properties.

- **Accurate Identification:** Look for the deeply lobed leaves with jagged edges, which radiate from the root in a rosette. The presence of a hollow stem with milky sap is another key identifier. When in doubt, consult a reliable field guide or foraging app to ensure accurate identification before consuming any wild plant.

- **Potential Look-alikes:** Dandelions are members of the sunflower family (Asteraceae), one of the most species-rich families of plants. Many plants in the family can resemble dandelions, several so closely that they are called "false dandelions", especially flatweeds (*Hypochaeris* spp.) and desert-chicory (*Pyrrhopappus* spp.). However, dandelions' hollow flowering stalks are unique to the genus and a reliable identifying feature.

Lamb's Quarters (*Chenopodium album*)

Lamb's quarters, also known as goosefoot, is another common denizen of disturbed areas, and a versatile edible green with a mild flavor and meaty texture quite similar to its more famous cousin, spinach (*Spinacia oleracea*). Its high nutritional value – especially its protein content – and hardiness make it a valuable potential food source.

Lamb's quarters (*Chenopodium album*).[88]

- **Distinct Characteristics:** Lamb's quarters have a fine white coating of hairs on their leaves and stems, especially on new growth, giving them a "dusty" or "floury" appearance. The leaves are triangular or diamond-shaped, somewhat similar in shape to a goose's webbed foot, with margins that are toothed distally (at the end furthest from the stem).

- **Preferred Habitats:** Similar to dandelions, lamb's quarters thrives in disturbed areas, including back yards, pastures, vacant lots, and roadsides. Its ability to tolerate poor (especially saline) soil conditions mean that it is often a pioneer plant, and one of the first species to colonize bare patches of ground.

- **Seasonal Nuances:** Young lamb's quarters leaves are most tender and flavorful in early spring. As the plant matures, the leaves become tougher and slightly bitter. However, even mature lamb's quarters leaves are enjoyed if blanched or cooked longer to soften their texture.

- **Nutritional Benefits:** Lamb's quarters are a good source of vitamins A, C, and K, as well as iron and calcium. It also contains protein and fiber, making it a well-rounded nutritional addition to your diet.

- **Accurate Identification:** Look for the floury white coating on the upper leaves and stems (often tinged red in older plants), along with the triangular or diamond-shaped leaves with partially toothed margins.

- **Potential Look-alikes:** Wild pigweed (*Amaranthus* spp.) and pokeweed (*Phytolacca americana*) have a similar overall appearance to lamb's quarters and may be mistaken for it. The leaves of wild pigweed are similar in appearance (and also edible), but lack the toothed margins of lamb's quarters. Pokeweed has larger leaves with smooth margins and produces dark blue or purple berries; the young greens are sometimes cooked and eaten as "poke salad", but all parts of the plant are toxic from early summer on. Always consult a reliable identification guide before consuming any wild plant, and never harvest anything you are unsure about.

Chickweed (*Stellaria media*)

Chickweed, a delicate yet fast-growing annual, is a welcome sight for foragers in early spring (and sometimes autumn). Its ability to thrive in cool, damp conditions make it a reliable source of fresh greens in the shoulder seasons.

Chickweed.[34]

- **Distinct Characteristics:** Chickweed has small, elliptical or spade-shaped leaves that grow in opposite pairs along a slender, often sprawling stem. The stems of chickweed usually have a distinctive line of hairs along one side, and if pulled apart will reveal a slightly elastic "core" in the center (some foragers jokingly call this the chickweed "bone"). The small white flowers have five petals, but because they are deeply cleft they can appear doubled, giving the appearance of tiny daisies.

- **Preferred Habitats:** Chickweed thrives in damp areas such as part-shade gardens, open woodlands, and even along roadsides. In good conditions, it can form dense mats, making it easily recognizable (and easy to harvest) in suitable habitats.

- **Seasonal Nuances:** Chickweed is a cool-season annual that thrives in early spring. In milder climates, some seeds will germinate in early fall, and these plants can be harvested throughout the winter. While plants may be found sporadically through mid-summer, especially in cooler microclimates, most will have withered and dried up by late spring.

- **Nutritional Benefits:** Chickweed is a good source of vitamins A and C, iron, and potassium. It also has a high water content, making it a refreshing addition to salads and stir-fries.

- **Accurate Identification:** Look for the dainty, oppositely-arranged leaves that look a little like spades (the card suit). Also look for the presence of a single line of hairs along one side of the stem, which reveals an elastic "core" when tugged gently apart: these traits are unique to chickweed and will prevent confusion with lookalikes.

- **Potential Look-alikes:** Because chickweed is relatively nondescript when not in bloom, it is easy to confuse with other cool-season annuals, like the common (and toxic) scarlet pimpernel (*Anagallis arvensis*). This makes it especially important to conclusively identify any plants you plan to eat. When in doubt, wait until the small – but distinctive – flowers open before harvesting.

By familiarizing yourself with these readily available and easily identifiable staple greens, you'll add a touch of wild flavor to your meals.

Profiles of Edible Flowers

Apart from the delicious greens and hearty nuts, the Northeast also has an array of edible flowers that add a touch of beauty and unexpected flavor to your dishes. However, before you head out with a basket in hand, learning about safe and accurate identification is crucial. Here, you explore three delightful edible flowers, including delicate violets (*Viola* spp.), fragrant elderflowers (*Sambucus nigra*), and surprisingly versatile daylilies (*Hemerocallis* spp.).

Violets (*Viola* spp.)

Violets, with their cheerful blooms peeking from beneath fallen leaves in early spring, are not just a symbol of springtime but also edible delights. Both the flowers and the leaves can be eaten raw or cooked, adding a mild, floral touch to salads, desserts, and even cocktails.

Common violets (*Viola sororia*).[35]

- **Distinct Characteristics:** Violets come in a variety of colors, with the most common being blue, purple, and white. All have flowers with five in a distinctive"two above, three below" pattern. The leaves of most species are heart-shaped, with scalloped edges and a smooth texture.

- **Preferred Habitats:** Most violet species thrive in shaded woodland areas with moist soil. They often carpet the forest floor in early spring, creating a breathtaking display of color. Some common species, like the marsh blue violet (*V. cucullata*), prefer open country, such as wet meadows and pastures.

- **Seasonal Nuances:** Violets are at their best and most abundant in early spring, when both flowers and leaves are fresh and tender. As the season progresses, the flowers fade, and the leaves may become tougher.

- **Nutritional Benefits:** Violets offer a surprising amount of vitamin C and are a good source of antioxidants. They are also a natural source of salicylic acid, a compound with anti-inflammatory properties.

- **Accurate Identification:** In early spring, look for the plants' distinctive heart-shaped leaves with scalloped edges, emerging directly from the ground on long petioles (leaf stalks). Consult a reliable field guide to differentiate between various violet species, as some may have slightly different flavors.

- **Potential Look-alikes:** Lesser celandine (*Ficaria verna*) can closely resemble violets when not in bloom, with similar heart-shaped leaves and a low, clumping growth habit. The leaves of lesser celandine have wavy rather than scalloped margins, but the yellow flowers are much more reliable; beginners should only harvest from plants that have begun blooming until they learn to recognize and distinguish the two plants.

Fun Fact: Violets were once a popular ingredient in candy. Queen Elizabeth I of England reportedly enjoyed violet-flavored candies, and candied violets were used to decorate cakes and desserts during the Victorian era.

Elderflowers (*Sambucus nigra*)

Elder, with its delicate white clusters of flowers, is a fragrant harbinger of summer. The blossoms and berries add a touch of floral sweetness to syrups, fritters, and even cocktails.

Elderflowers.[36]

- **Distinct Characteristics:** Elder is a multi-trunked shrub, often producing "suckers" from the roots and forming dense thickets in good soils. The leaves are oppositely arranged on the stem and pinnately compound, with each leaf composed of several oval-shaped leaflets arranged along a central stalk or *rachis*. The tiny, white flowers emerge in spring in large, flat clusters, which are replaced by deep purplish-black fruits by autumn.

- **Preferred Habitats:** Elderflowers prefer moist soil and full sun. They grow wild along roadsides, stream and river banks, and abandoned fields, and can become aggressive in good conditions, forming large single-species colonies.

- **Seasonal Nuances:** Elderflowers are at their peak in late spring to early summer. Once the flowers begin to wither, it's too late to harvest them -- but the berries can be harvested in late summer or autumn when they ripen to a glossy dark purple or black.

- **Nutritional Benefits:** Elderflowers are a good source of antioxidants and have been used traditionally for their immune-boosting properties. They are also high in flavonoids, which are believed to offer various health benefits.

- **Accurate Identification:** Look for large, flat-topped clusters of tiny white florets. The leaves are a key identifier, pinnately compound and oppositely arranged on the stem.

Potential Look-Alikes: Ash trees have leaves that are both opposite and compound, like those of elder; however, their flowers are inconspicuous and their fruits are papery samaras similar to maple seeds. Of more concern to beginners is the toxic water hemlock (*Cicuta* spp.), which has compound leaves and large white clusters of flowers that give it a striking, if superficial, similarity to elder. However, water hemlock's leaves are alternately arranged, and it is a herbaceous plant -- dying back to the ground each winter -- whereas elder is a woody plant.

Fun Fact: Elderflowers have been used for centuries in traditional medicine. The ancient Egyptians used elderflowers to treat wounds, while the Greeks believed they could improve eyesight.

Daylilies (*Hemerocallis* spp.)

Daylilies, with their vivid orange, yellow, or red blooms, might surprise you with their edible potential. While not all lily varieties are safe to consume, certain species offer delicious flowers and buds used in various culinary creations. Unlike most flowers that bloom for days or even weeks, daylilies, as their name suggests, only open for a single day. This fleeting beauty makes their culinary use even more special.

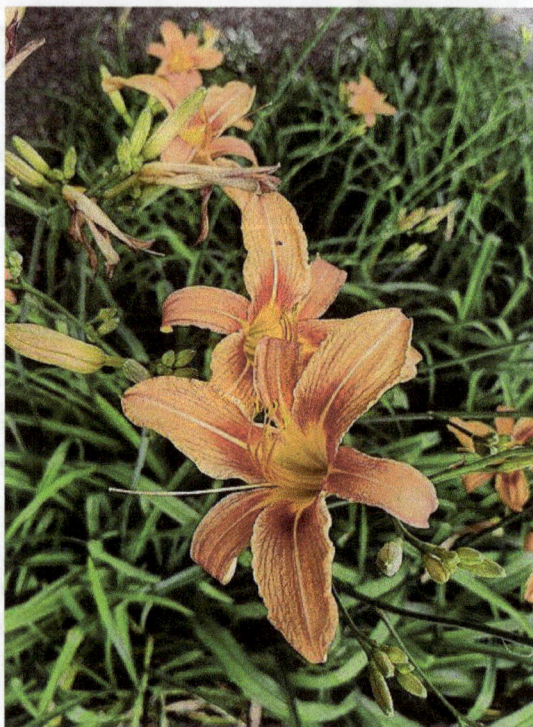

Daylilies (*Hemerocallis fulva*).[87]

- **Distinct Characteristics:** Daylilies have long, grass-like leaves and large, trumpet-shaped flowers with six petals, which are borne on long, thin stalks and – true to their name – last for only a day or two, though they may bloom intermittently throughout the year. They come in various colors, including orange, yellow, red, and even purple, but not all are safe to eat: generally speaking, only wild-growing daylilies with orange flowers (*Hemerocallis fulva*) should be harvested if intended for consumption. Always consult a reliable resource to identify the specific daylily species before incorporating them into your diet.

- **Preferred Habitats:** Daylilies are not native to North America, but have proven themselves quite adaptable; they thrive in a variety of conditions, from full sun to partial shade and moist to fairly dry soils. Originally introduced as ornamental garden plants, they have escaped and naturalized, and can be found in floodplains, pastures, roadsides, and other disturbed areas.

- **Seasonal Nuances:** Daylily flowers and buds are best enjoyed in early summer when they are fresh and vibrant. As the name suggests, the flowers last only a day or two, withering soon after. The edible tubers, which can be cooked and eaten like potatoes, are best harvested in spring or early fall, before or after the plants have flowered.

- **Nutritional Benefits:** Daylily flowers and buds offer a good source of vitamins A and C and antioxidants. They are also a low-calorie and fat-free ingredient, making them a guilt-free way to add a touch of color and flavor to your dishes.

- **Accurate Identification:** Look for trumpet-shaped flowers with six petals and consult a reliable guide specifically focused on identifying edible daylily varieties. Many daylily cultivars bred for ornamental purposes are not recommended for consumption.

- **Potential Look-alikes:** Hybrid and ornamental varieties of daylily may not be safe to eat, so only harvest wild plants with orange or red flowers. Other plants in the lily family, especially true lilies (*Lillium* spp.), may also be toxic and should be avoided if you cannot identify them conclusively.

Fun Fact: Daylilies are incredibly versatile and have been used for centuries not just as ornamentals but also for medicinal purposes. The flower buds were traditionally used as a styptic to stop bleeding, while the roots were believed to have anti-inflammatory properties.

Moderation is key to any edible flower. Start with small quantities and monitor your body's reaction, especially if you have any allergies. By familiarizing yourself with these flavorful options, you'll add a touch of floral flair to your culinary creations and celebrate the beauty and bounty of the Northeast's edible flowers.

Profiles of Wild Berries

Summer in the Northeast explodes with eye-catching colors, and a significant portion of this stunning display comes from the abundance of wild berries. These juicy delights offer a delicious reward for the adventurous forager, bursting with flavor and packed with essential nutrients. However, proper identification is crucial, as some wild berry look-alikes are toxic. Here, you'll discover three iconic wild berries of the Northeast, including the beloved blueberry, the tangy raspberry, and the robust blackberry.

Blueberry (*Vaccinium* spp.)

The blueberry, a quintessential symbol of summer in the Northeast, needs little introduction. These sweet and versatile berries are perfect for eating fresh, baking into pies and muffins, or transforming into jams and jellies.

"Wild" or "lowbush" blueberry (*Vaccinium angustifolium*).[38]

- **Distinct Characteristics:** Blueberries are small, round berries with a smooth, waxy coating, produced by a number of shrubs in the genus *Vaccinium*, especially *V. corymbosum* (highbush blueberry) and *V. angustifolium* (lowbush or wild blueberry). Their color ranges from a light blue to a deep, almost indigo purple when fully ripe, often with a grayish cast due to the coating on the berry's skin. The flowers are tiny, white, and bell-shaped, and the leaves are generally elliptical, either broad and smooth-edged (highbush) or narrower and with finely serrated edges (lowbush). The leaves are often conspicuously spotted with what looks like rust, actually a pathogenic fungus.

- **Preferred Habitats:** Blueberries thrive in acidic soils and are commonly found in moist woodlands, bogs, and marshes. In ideal conditions, they can form dense and extensive "blueberry barrens".

- **Seasonal Nuances:** Blueberries ripen in mid to late summer, depending on the specific variety and location. The berries are at their peak when they are plump but slightly yielding and dark blue or purple.

- **Nutritional Benefits:** Blueberries are a powerhouse of antioxidants and are well-known for their potential health benefits. They are also a good source of vitamin C, fiber, and manganese.

- **Accurate Identification:** In spring, look for clusters of small, white flowers on low- to medium-sized shrubs in open areas. As the summer wears on, keep an eye out for the round berries, often with a waxy coating and a red, purple, or blue color beneath. Consult a reliable field guide to differentiate between various blueberry species, as some may have slightly different flavors.

- **Potential Look-alikes:** Cranberries (*V. oxycoccos* and other species) are closely related to blueberries, and can often be found in similar habitats. They are also edible, but the berries are red when ripe instead of blue-purple. Be cautious of mistaking blueberries for baneberry (*Actaea* spp.) or pokeweed (*Phytolacca americana*). Both of these plants produce dark-colored berries that are highly toxic and cause serious illness if ingested. Baneberry leaves are trifoliolate, meaning each leaf has three leaflets (like poison ivy), while blueberry leaves are simple. Pokeweed is an annual, while blueberries are woody shrubs; its leaves are also much larger and more flexible than blueberry leaves. When in doubt, always err on the side of caution and leave the berry unidentified.

Fun Fact: Blueberries weren't always a popular fruit. Native American tribes were the first to appreciate their culinary and medicinal value, but European settlers initially considered them bland and uninteresting food. Thankfully, their deliciousness eventually won over even the most skeptical palates.

Raspberry (*Rubus idaeus*)

With their stark red color and sweet-tart flavor, raspberries are a delightful summer treat. These delicate berries grow on prickly canes, adding a touch of excitement (and perhaps a few scratches) to the foraging experience.

Raspberry.[39]

- **Distinct Characteristics:** Raspberries are unmistakable, formed of numerous tiny indibidual fruits and often with a soft, velvety or hairy texture. Their color ranges from a bright red to a deep crimson when fully ripe. The flowers are white, about a half inch long, and five-petaled, with many conspicuous stamens at the center. Raspberry leaves are compound, with serrated edges and a light green color. The leaves and stems are covered in prickles, so wear gloves when harvesting.

- **Preferred Habitats:** Raspberries thrive in disturbed areas with full to partial sun. They are found along forest edges, roadsides, and abandoned fields. Look for thickets of prickly canes with clusters of red berries dangling from the branches.

- **Seasonal Nuances:** Raspberries typically ripen in early to mid-summer, depending on the specific variety and location. The berries are at their peak when they are plump, bright red, and detach easily from the cane. Unripe raspberries are not suitable to eat but were used medicinally by Native Americans and early settlers to treat stomach upset.

- **Nutritional Benefits:** Raspberries are an excellent source of vitamin C, fiber, and manganese. They also contain antioxidants and are believed to offer various health benefits, including potentially reducing inflammation and improving heart health.

- **Accurate Identification:** Look for the small, red, hairy berries growing on prickly canes. Consult a reliable field guide to differentiate between wild raspberries and cultivated varieties. Wild raspberries tend to be smaller and slightly tarter than their cultivated counterparts.

- **Potential Look-alikes:** Raspberries are members of a genus (*Rubus*) with dozens, perhaps hundreds of species, many of them very difficult to distinguish. All are edible, but raspberries can be distinguished by their stems and leaves, which are not only prickly but densely hairy at the tips, and frequently have a reddish tinge.

Fun Fact: The scientific name for raspberries, *Rubus idaeus*, comes from the Latin word "rubus," which means "bramble," and "idaeus," meaning "from Mount Ida" -- a mountain in Greece where raspberries were said to have been abundant in ancient times. Legend has it that Zeus, the king of the Greek gods, brought raspberries to Mount Ida as food for his infant son so the berries would be plentiful and easy for the child to reach.

Blackberry (*Rubus* spp.)

Blackberries are another summer favorite for foragers with their deep purple-to-black color and robust flavor. These juicy berries grow in clusters along prickly canes, offering a rewarding harvest for those willing to brave a few thorns.

Blackberry.[40]

- **Distinct Characteristics:** Blackberries are similar in shape to raspberries but are larger and have a darker color. They are round to slightly oblong with smooth, glossy skin. When fully ripe, the berries should be a deep purple or black and detach easily from the cane. The leaves are compound, with 3 or 5 leaflets; each leaflet has serrated edges and a light green color. The stems or canes are usually armed with prickles (though the size and density of prickles depends on the species), so wear gloves when harvesting.

- **Preferred Habitats:** Blackberries thrive in disturbed areas with full to partial sun. They are found along forest edges, roadsides, and abandoned fields. Look for thickets of prickly canes with clusters of white flowers or dark-colored berries dangling from the branches.

- **Seasonal Nuances:** Blackberries ripen mid to late summer, depending on the specific variety and location. The berries are at their peak when plump, have a deep purple-black color, and fall off the cane easily. Avoid blackberries that are still red or green, as they will be tart and unpleasant to eat.

- **Nutritional Benefits:** Blackberries are an excellent source of vitamin C, fiber, and manganese. They are also rich in antioxidants, including anthocyanins, which are believed to offer various health benefits, such as improving brain function and reducing the risk of heart disease.

- **Accurate Identification:** Look for the sprawling, prickly canes in fall or early spring, which will bloom abundantly with white flowers in mid-spring. Consult a reliable field guide to differentiate between various blackberry species, as some may have slightly different flavors and textures.

- **Potential Look-alikes:** Blackberries, raspberries, and other brambles produce unique multiple fruits that are found in no species outside the genus. The fruits of all species of *Rubus* are edible, though they're not all as delicious as the most popular species. Mulberries (*Morus* spp.) are superficially similar, though in fact they aren't closely related; mulberries appear on trees, while brambles are herbaceous and do not form wood. Always ensure the berries are ripe, and consult a field guide if unsure.

Fun Fact: Blackberries were once considered a symbol of purity and innocence. In ancient Celtic cultures, blackberries were associated with the goddess Brigid, who represented creativity, healing, and poetry. Blackberries were also used in traditional medicine to treat a variety of ailments, including coughs, stomach upset, and wounds.

By familiarizing yourself with these descriptions and exercising caution when foraging, you'll enjoy the delicious bounty of wild berries. Prepare to transform your summer outings into delightful foraging adventures punctuated by the sweet rewards of these wild berry treasures.

Profiles of Nuts and Seeds

As summer wanes and autumn paints the Northeast landscape in colorful hues, another chapter unfolds in the forager's story. This season ushers in clusters of nuts and seeds, bursting with energy and a satisfying reward for a successful harvest. However, foraging for wild nuts and seeds requires knowledge and caution. Here, you'll explore four common options: ubiquitous acorn, flavorful hickory nut, elusive pine nut, and robust black walnut.

Acorns (*Quercus* spp.)

Acorns, the quintessential symbol of fall, are more than just crunchy trinkets beneath towering oak trees. For time out of mind, they have been valued as a staple food by peoples in both the Old World and the New.

Leaves and acorns of the common white oak (*Quercus alba*), a lower-tannin species suitable for eating. Note the veins on the leaves, which extend to the tips of the lobes but not past them.[41]

- **Distinct Characteristics:** Acorns vary in size and shape as much as the species that produce them, but are generally ovoid or oblong. One end is enclosed in a hard, scaly "cap" or *cupule*, and the kernel within ranges from nearly white to yellow or brown. Most are about the size of a quarter or smaller, but the bur oak (*Q. macrocarpa*) produces mild-flavored acorns that reach the size of golf balls!

- **Preferred Habitats:** Oaks are among the most abundant and dominant trees throughout eastern North America, and major constituents of woodlands and forests, savannas, and even urban areas. In the Northeast, the common white oak (*Q. alba*), Northern red oak (*Q. rubra*), chinkapin oak (*Q. muehlenbergii*), and black oak (*Q. velutina*) are among the most common of the twenty or so species native to the region.

- **Seasonal Nuances:** Acorns start falling in late summer and continue throughout autumn and into winter. However, not all fallen acorns are ready for consumption. The cap of a ripe acorn should detach easily from the nut, and the shell should be brown, not green. Watch out for acorns with cracks or holes in the shells, as these are almost certainly either moldy or worm-infested. However, some foragers will tell you that recently sprouted acorns taste the best (you can do this at home in a bucket of damp sand), as the starches in the kernel are converted to sugar to fuel the seedling's growth.

- **Nutritional Benefits:** Acorns are a good source of carbohydrates, healthy fats, and fiber. They also contain essential minerals like potassium, magnesium, and iron. However, acorns should always be thoroughly cooked before consuming, both to prevent food-borne illness and to remove any tannins.

- **Accurate Identification:** In general, the acorns of so-called "white oaks" (subg. *Quercus*) have a milder flavor and lower concentrations of bitter tannins than the "red oaks" (subg. Lobatae). The two groups are fairly easy to distinguish, even when the exact species is unknown: the leaves of red oaks have veins that extend past the margins of the leaves forming sharp bristles, while the leaves of white oaks do not. The shells of red oak acorns are also usually woolly or hairy inside, while white oak acorn shells are smooth within.

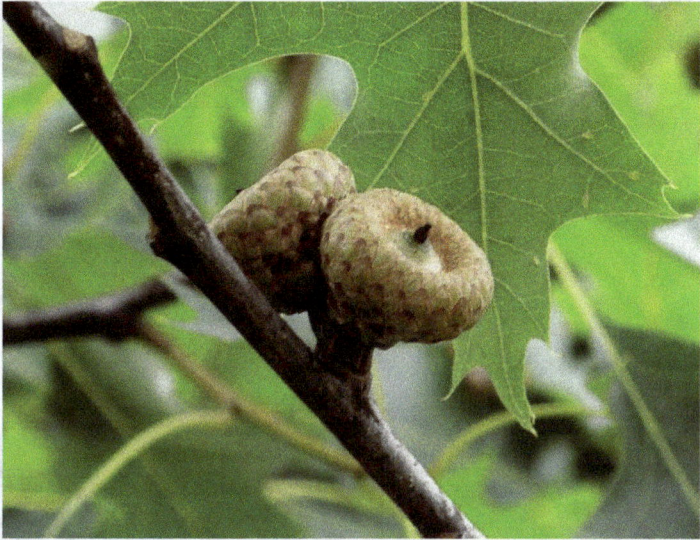

Leaves and immature acorns of the Northern red oak (*Q. rubra*), a high-tannin species. Note the sharp, "bristly" tips of the leaf lobes, formed by leaf veins extending beyond the tips.[48]

- **Potential Look-Alikes:** No trees other than oaks produce acorn-like fruits, so the biggest danger when harvesting acorns is accidentally harvesting from a species with bitter acorns. Although it's no fun, even bitter acorns are safe to eat (or at least taste) if they have been cooked, so don't be afraid to try new species, as long as you harvest and process the acorns safely.

Fun Fact: Acorns have played a significant role in human history. Acorns were a staple food in cultures as diverse as ancient Greece and Bronze Age Japan, not to mention indigenous peoples across North America from the Navajo to the Iroquois. In many of these cultures, acorns continue to be an important part of traditional cuisine: Koreans even make a kind of tofu from acorns called *dotori-muk*.

Hickory Nuts (*Carya* spp.)

Hickory nuts are closely related to pecans (*Carya illinoensis*), but their edible nuts, which are encased in a thick husk, are a unique and delicious reward for the patient forager. They have a rich, buttery flavor that can be enjoyed raw, cooked, or even pureed: long before today's health food fads, Native Americans were making and drinking nut milk from hickory nuts, which the American naturalist William Bartram (1739-1823) claimed was "as sweet and rich as fresh cream". Like oaks, not all hickory species produce equally delicious nuts: some, often called "pignut" hickories, are too bitter to be palatable.

Leaves and unripe nuts of the shagbark hickory (*Carya ovata*), one of the most common and highly regarded species.[48]

- **Distinct Characteristics:** Hickory trees are related to pecans, and are in the same family as walnuts (*Juglans* spp.), and are superficially similar to both: they have compound leaves (usually with 5, 7, or 9 leaflets) that emit a strong and distinctive smellwhen crushed or bruised, and produce nuts encased in thick husks. Like pecans, hickory husks are divided into four sections, but they are much thicker than pecan husks. In the Northeast, the shagbark hickory (*C. ovata*) is among the most abundant species, and is easily recognized by its shaggy, exfoliating bark.

- **Preferred Habitats:** Hickory trees generally prefer moist, well-drained soils, and are often dominant or co-dominant species in eastern hardwood forests, especially in river valleys. Look for them along rivers and streams, floodplains, and south-facing slopes, especially further north.

- **Seasonal Nuances:** Hickory nuts mature in late summer and fall. The husks will turn brown when the nuts are ripe; mmature nuts will be difficult to open and are quite bitter. Avoid any nuts with cracks in the hard brown inner shell, or with shriveled or discolored kernels.

- **Nutritional Benefits:** Hickory nuts are a good source of healthy fats, protein, and fiber. They also contain essential minerals like manganese, magnesium, and phosphorus. Hickory nuts are a high-calorie food, making them a great source of energy.

- **Accurate Identification:** One of the most common and best-tasting species of hickory is the shagbark hickory, which is easily identified by its large size and "shaggy" bark, often hanging in strips from the trunk; the leaves of shagbark are nearly always 5-compound, though other species may have more or fewer leaflets.

- **Potential Look-Alikes:** Pecans (*C. illinoensis*) are closely related, but have much thinner husks. Walnuts (*Juglans* spp.) resemble nearly spherical hickory nuts, but their husks are even thicker and lack obvious segmentation. All species of hickory and walnut are edible, though some are unpalatably bitter. Buckeyes or horse chestnuts (*Aesculus glabra*) also come from large trees and are enclosed in husks that split on maturity, and are worth mentioning because they are toxic. However, the husks of buckeyes are spiny, and the kernels are a deep glossy brown, while hickory nuts have smooth husks and have light brown kernels.

Fun Fact: Hickory nuts were a significant food source for Native American tribes in the Northeast. They used hickory nuts for food and medicine, and the wood for tools, buildings, and ornaments.

Pine Nuts (*Pinus* spp.)

Pine nuts, with their buttery flavor and versatility, are a coveted find for foragers. However, note that not all pine cones produce edible nuts. Here, you'll discover two commercially available varieties found in the Northeast: Eastern white pine (Pinus strobus) and Korean pine (Pinus koraiensis).

Black Walnut (*Juglans nigra*)

Black walnut trees look like a lot like their cousins in the family Juglandaceae, hickory (*Carya* spp.) and pecan (*C. illinoensis*) trees, and their nuts look a *bit* like small, gnarly hickory nuts or pecans. Walnut husks are thicker than pecan or hickory husks, and don't split open when ripe. Freeing the meat takes a little work – but the reward is a delicious nut with a unique taste that complements many dishes.

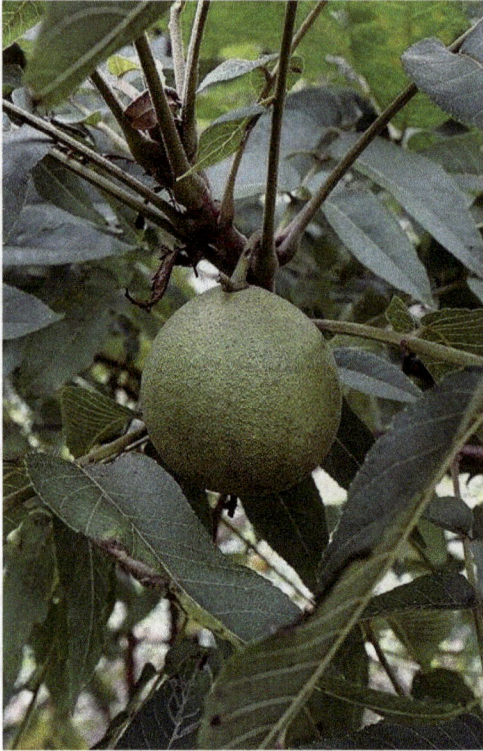

Black walnut (*Juglans nigra*)."

- **Distinct Characteristics:** Black walnut trees are similar in appearance to pecans and hickories, with compound leaves comprising 9 to 21 leaflets, which emit a pungent, slightly spicy smell when crushed. The nuts are spherical, encased in a thick, green husk that will stain your fingers brown if you handle it too much. The nut itself quite small compared to the surrounding husk, with a wrinkly or ridged brown shell and a kernel similar in appearance to a pecan or store-bought walnut, though much smaller.

- **Preferred Habitats:** Black walnut trees thrive in rich, moist soils and are commonly found in floodplains, bottomlands, and mixed hardwood forests throughout the Northeast. Look for large, stately trees with fallen husks littering the ground in the fall.

- **Seasonal Nuances:** Black walnuts mature in late summer to early fall. The husks will turn brown and begin to split open when the nuts are ready for harvest. Avoid picking immature nuts, as they will be difficult to crack and have a less desirable flavor.

- **Nutritional Benefits:** Black walnuts are an excellent source of healthy fats, protein, and fiber. They are also rich in antioxidants and essential minerals like manganese, magnesium, and copper. Black walnuts are a high-calorie food, making them a great source of energy.

- **Accurate Identification:** Look for fallen nuts beginning in early autumn: their distinctive, thick green husks should easily mark them out from other types of nuts. Consulting a reliable field guide will further solidify your identification.

- **Potential Look-Alikes:** Black walnuts are sometimes confused with the butternut (*J. cinerea*), a closely related species which has declined due to a fungus commonly called *butternut canker*, which was introduced to North America from Asia in the early 20th century. Butternuts are oblong – more like pecans than black walnuts – but are otherwise quite similar. Although they are also edible, it's best to leave any butternuts you find, as the species needs all the new recruits it can get.

Fun Fact: Black walnut trees were prized by Native American tribes for their edible nuts and their medicinal properties. The leaves and hulls of black walnuts were used to treat a variety of ailments, including skin conditions and digestive problems. Black walnut wood is also highly prized for its beauty and durability, and it has been used for centuries in furniture making and other woodworking applications.

Profiles of Roots and Tubers

The Northeast's foraging landscape extends beyond the realm of fruits, nuts, and seeds. Beneath the surface lies a hidden buffet of roots and tubers, offering a rewarding harvest for the adventurous forager. However, proper identification is crucial, as some underground plant parts are toxic. Here, you explore three fascinating examples, including the long and versatile burdock, the surprisingly edible cattail, and the wild ancestor of the cultivated carrot.

Burdock (*Arctium lappa*)

Burdock, often overlooked as a weed, has a long history as a culinary and medicinal plant. Its long taproot is a delicious and nutritious addition to stir-fries, soups, and stews, while the young leaves are enjoyed in salads or cooked greens. Burdock has been cultivated for food and medicinal purposes in Asia for centuries, but has naturalized throughout northern North America, from Portland, OR to Portland, ME.

Burdock (*Arctium lappa*).⁴⁴

- **Distinct Characteristics:** Burdock is a biennial with enormous, heart-shaped green leaves. These stay in a leafy rosette in the first year, but grow quite tall in the second spring, producing their distinctive burr-like flower heads atop stalks that may reach eight feet high or higher! These burrs are equipped with tiny hooks that readily cling to clothing or animal fur, aiding in seed dispersal. The root is long and tapered, with black or brown "skin" surrounding white flesh inside.

- **Preferred Habitats:** Burdock thrives in sunny, disturbed areas throughout northern North America . It can be found along roadsides, old pastures and cropland, and even vacant lots. Look for its large (up to two feet long) heart-shaped green leaves with long, fleshy petioles (stalks) somewhat like those of Swiss chard.

- **Seasonal Nuances:** Burdock root should be harvested in the first fall or winter, after the plant has had some time to grow but before it bolts. The root becomes dry, woody and bland after the plant flowers, as most of the carbohydrates stored within it have been used up. However, the flower stalks themselves can be peeled and cooked, with a flavor and texture somewhat like artichoke hearts, while the young leaves can be harvested throughout spring and early summer and cooked like chard or kale.

- **Nutritional Benefits:** Burdock root is a good source of fiber, inulin (a prebiotic that promotes gut health), and essential minerals like potassium and iron. It also contains antioxidants and anti-inflammatory compounds. Inulin is a type of dietary fiber that feeds the beneficial bacteria in your gut, promoting digestive health and potentially boosting the immune system. Some studies have also suggested that burdock root may have anti-cancer properties, although more research is needed.

- **Accurate Identification:** Look for the elephantine green leaves in spring, and the distinctive burr-like flower heads in summer. Although blooming plants shouldn't be harvested fror their roots, they can for their young leaves and stalks, and there's a good chance that some first-year plants are growing nearby. Consult a reliable field guide to differentiate burdock from other look-alikes. When in doubt, it's always best to err on the side of caution and leave the plant unidentified.

- **Potential Look-Alikes:** True to its name, burdock can sometimes be confused with some species of dock (*Rumex* spp.), especially curly dock (*R. crispus*). Although not closely related, dock also has large, fleshy leaves and a long taproot like burtdock; however, dock leaves *never* reach the huge size of burdock leaves, and their flowers are tiny and inconspicuous.

Fun Fact: Burdock has been used in traditional medicine for centuries. The roots, leaves, and seeds have been used to treat various ailments, including skin conditions, coughs, and digestive problems. In Japan, burdock root (gobo) is a popular and versatile vegetable used in many traditional dishes. Burdock root is often julienned and stir-fried or braised until tender, adding a satisfyingly chewy texture and earthy flavor to meals.

Cattail (*Typha* spp.)

Cattails, with their tall, slender stalks and distinctive brown spikes, are common in wetlands and marshes nearly worldwide. While they may not be the first plant to come to mind when considering edible foraged foods, the young shoots and root stalks of cattails offer a surprising culinary adventure. Cattail hearts, the tender white cores of the young shoots, are eaten raw, cooked, or pickled, while the root stalks are roasted or boiled for a starchy and slightly sweet flavor. The flowers can also be steamed or boiled and eaten like baby corn.

Cattails.[46]

- **Distinct Characteristics:** Cattails are tall, perennial plants that thrive in wet environments. They have very long, slender, green leaves with a firm, spongy texture, emerging from a thick, underground rhizome. The most recognizable feature is the brown, sausage-shaped flower spike that appears at the top of the stalk in early summer. This spike matures into a fluffy white "tail" later in the season.

- **Preferred Habitats:** Cattails are nearly always found near or in still water: marshes, swamps, ponds, and even stock tanks and human-made reservoirs are all suitable habitats. Even desert environments can host the plants Look for dense stands of tall plants with the characteristic brown spikes or white fluffy tails.

- **Seasonal Nuances:** The edible parts of cattails are best harvested in the spring and early summer, before or just after the plants flower. The young shoots, or cattail hearts, are most tender during this time. As the season progresses, the shoots become tougher and less palatable, and the flowers become inedible. The root stalks can be harvested year-round, but they are generally at their best in the fall and winter after the starches have had a chance to develop.

- **Nutritional Benefits:** Cattail hearts and root stalks are a good source of carbohydrates, fiber, and vitamin C. They are also low-calorie foods, making them a good choice for those who are watching their weight. Additionally, cattail pollen has been used traditionally for its medicinal properties, although more research is needed to confirm its effectiveness.

- **Accurate Identification:** Look for tall plants with very long (up to 6 feet), slender leaves with a spongy texture, as well as the distinctive brown flower spikes or white fluffy tails. Consult a reliable field guide to ensure you are identifying cattail (*Typha* spp.) and not another wetland plant.

- **Potential Look-Alikes:** Three species of cattail are native to the United States; they are similar in appeareance, but all are edible. The yellow flag (*Iris pseudoacorus*) and other species of iris are often found in similar habitats, and all are toxic. Their leaves and shoots are flat, shorter than cattails, and lack cattails' spongy texture; they also produce showy blooms completely unlike the inconspicuous wind-pollinated flowers of cattails.

Fun Fact: Cattails have played a significant role in human history across various cultures. Native American tribes used cattails for food, medicine, and even building materials. The fluffy cattail "tails" were used for stuffing pillows and mattresses, while the long leaves were woven into baskets and mats.

Wild Carrot (Daucus carota)

The wild carrot, often mistaken for a common weed, is the unrefined ancestor of the cultivated carrot you enjoy today. While its roots are not as large or plump as their domesticated counterparts, they offer a unique and slightly bitter flavor that's appreciated in stir-fries, soups, or roasted. The young leaves and flower heads are also used in salads or as a garnish for a touch of wild carrot essence.

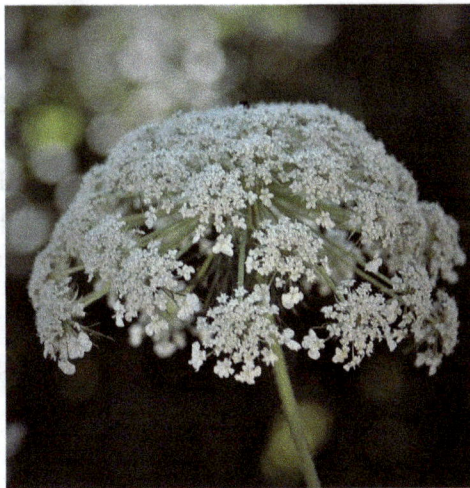

Wild carrot.[47]

- **Distinct Characteristics:** Wild carrots resemble their cultivated cousins, with feathery green leaves that are finely divided and lacy in appearance. The flower clusters are round-topped umbels with numerous small white flowers. In bud, the umbels may appear pinkish, and often have a single reddish or purple flower in the center. As the flowers mature, the umbels fold inwards and become slightly concave, resembling a bird's nest. Unlike cultivated carrots, wild carrot roots are smaller, spindly, and have a creamy white or light yellow color.

- **Preferred Habitats:** Wild carrots thrive in disturbed areas with full to partial sun. They are found in meadows, fields, roadsides, and even wastelands. Look for tall plants with ferny leaves and flat, white flower clusters.

- **Seasonal Nuances:** Wild carrots are biennials, meaning they spend the first year in a rosette and bloom the second spring before dying. Only the roots of first-year plants are palatable, so locate these in the summer before harvesting in the fall and early winter, around the time of the first frost. (The frost mellows out the bitterness of the roots, making them more palatable.) Young leaves and flower heads can be harvested throughout the spring and early summer.

- **Nutritional Benefits:** Wild carrots offer a similar nutritional profile to their cultivated counterparts. They are a good source of vitamins A and C, fiber, and essential minerals like potassium and manganese.

- **Accurate Identification:** Because blooming plants are more conspicuous, locate these and find first-year rosettes among them. Look for the ferny green leaves and the round-topped, white flower clusters with a single, reddish, or purple flower in the center. Consult a reliable field guide to differentiate wild carrots from other members of the Apiaceae family, such as poison hemlock (*Conium maculatum*), which has a similar appearance but is highly toxic.

- **Potential Look-Alikes:** Be extremely cautious of poison hemlock (*Conium maculatum*). Poison hemlock has smooth, hairless stems and fern-like leaves with a glossy sheen, while wild carrot leaves are more feathery and have a hairy or bristly texture.

When in doubt, always err on the side of caution and leave the plant unidentified.

Fun Fact: Wild carrots were once cultivated for their aromatic leaves and seeds rather than their roots. The ancient Greeks and Romans used wild carrots for medicinal purposes, believing they possessed healing properties. Over time, selective breeding led to the development of the larger, sweeter-tasting carrots you know and love today. However, the wild carrot continues to thrive, offering a connection to your food's origins and a delicious flavor experience for the adventurous forager.

As you reach the end of this exploration into the wild edibles of the Northeast, you can confidently say that the natural world offers a surprising bounty beyond the familiar aisles of the supermarket. From the sweet burst of berries to the earthy richness of roots and tubers, foraging presents an opportunity to connect with nature, expand your culinary repertoire, and appreciate the diverse flavors of the Northeast.

Chapter 5: Mushrooms and Fungi of the Northeast

Fungi are the unsung heroes of the Northeast's forests. Far from mere decomposers, they create intricate partnerships with trees, forming mycorrhizal networks that fuel forest health. These unseen architects break down organic matter, returning nutrients to the soil and completing the cycle of life. However, fungi's wonders extend above ground. The mushrooms you see, their fruiting bodies, represent a stunning array of shapes, sizes, and colors. Some grace your table, while others hold medicinal promise or light up the forest floor with bioluminescence.

Fungi growing on a stump.[48]

This chapter unlocks the fascinating nuances of Northeast fungi. You'll explore their ecological significance and discover this region's captivating diversity of mushrooms. Detailed profiles will equip you to safely identify common edible and inedible species, transforming you from an observer to an informed explorer of this hidden kingdom. Prepare to be surprised and intrigued as you embark on this fungal foray.

The Mushroom's Makeup

Unlike plants, mushrooms lack chlorophyll and cannot produce their food. They are the fruiting bodies of fungi, a vast and diverse kingdom with a complex underground network of threads called mycelium. This hidden network is the true body of the fungus, silently working its magic in the soil, decomposing organic matter, and forming symbiotic relationships with plants. The mushroom, the part you see above ground, has the primary purpose of spore dispersal, ensuring the fungus's survival and propagation.

Key Anatomical Features

- **Cap (Pileus):** The umbrella-shaped or rounded top of the mushroom. This is the most visually different part, displaying a wide range of colors, textures, and shapes (bell-shaped, conical, flat, etc.). It's important to note that some mushrooms lack caps entirely, resembling morels or puffballs.

- **Gills (Lamellae):** Located on the underside of the cap, these thin, plate-like structures produce spores. Gills come in various colors (white, yellow, brown, black, even blue or green), spacing (closely spaced, distant), and attachment styles (decurrent, adnate, free), all crucial for identification. Some mushrooms, like boletes, have pores instead of gills on the underside of the cap.

- **Stipe (Stem):** The stalk that supports the cap. It can be central, off-center, or even absent in some species. The stipe can be smooth, rough, hollow, or solid and may have distinctive features like rings or scales. Some mushrooms have a bulbous base at the bottom of the stipe, which can be another helpful identification characteristic.

- **Veil (Universal and Partial):** A thin layer of tissue that can partially or fully cover the cap and/or stipe in young mushrooms. As the mushroom matures, the veil tears, sometimes leaving remnants like a ring on the stipe (universal veil) or patches on the cap (partial veil). Not all mushrooms have veils, but their presence or absence can be a key identification point.

Understanding Terminology

- **Spore Print:** Spores are fungi's reproductive units, similar to plants' seeds. A spore print will be produced by placing the cap of a mature mushroom on paper (gill side down) and leaving it undisturbed for a few hours. The color and shape of the spore print are essential identification clues. Common spore print colors include white, brown, black, pink, and purple.

- **Decurrent:** Gills that extend down the stipe beyond the point of attachment, like running down the stem.

- **Adnate:** Gills that are directly attached to the stipe with no space in between.

- **Free Gills:** Gills that are attached to the stipe but do not extend down onto it.

- **Mycelium:** The vegetative network of fungal threads that lives underground, decomposing organic matter, absorbing nutrients, and forming mycorrhizal relationships with plant roots.

- **Mycorrhiza:** A mutually beneficial relationship between a fungus and the roots of a plant. The fungus helps the plant absorb nutrients and water from the soil, while the plant provides the fungus with sugars produced through photosynthesis. This symbiotic association is vital for the health of many forest ecosystems.

The Importance of Accurate Identification

The Northeast boasts a stunning variety of mushrooms, but not all are safe to eat. Some can cause mild stomach upset, while others can be deadly poisonous. Confusing an edible species with a toxic look-alike can have serious consequences. This is why accurate identification is vital when foraging for wild mushrooms.

Safety First

- **Consult Reliable Field Guides:** Invest in a reputable field guide specifically focused on wild mushrooms of the Northeast. These guides provide detailed descriptions, photographs, and identification tips for various species. Look for guides with high-quality photographs and clear descriptions of key anatomical features.

- **Learn from Experienced Foragers:** Consider joining an expert-led guided mushroom foraging tour to learn identification skills in a safe and controlled environment. Look for tours led by experienced mycologists or naturalists who can teach you the basics of safe foraging practices.

- **Start Slow and Focus on a Few Easily Identifiable Species:** Don't overwhelm yourself by trying to learn too many mushrooms at once. Begin by focusing on a few common and easily identifiable edible species, such as chanterelles or morels. As your knowledge and confidence grow, you can gradually expand your repertoire.

By familiarizing yourself with basic mushroom anatomy, terminology, and safe foraging practices, you'll unlock the secrets of Northeast mushrooms with confidence and appreciation. The journey of learning about wild mushrooms is a lifelong pursuit. Embrace the challenge, prioritize safety, and embark on a rewarding exploration of this fascinating kingdom.

Tips and Techniques for Safe Mushroom Identification

The thrill of discovering a hidden patch of mushrooms in the forest can be exhilarating. However, the excitement should never overshadow the importance of safe identification. Here, you delve into key techniques to distinguish between edible, inedible, and poisonous mushrooms so you can navigate Northeast fungi confidently.

Spore-bearing surface under cap

Gills:
wide and thin sheet-like
plates radiating from stem

Pores:
many small tubes ending
in a spongy surface

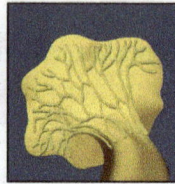

Ridges:
short, blunt elevated lines
on stem and under cap

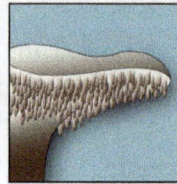

Teeth:
many small finger-like
projections

Gill attachment

Adnate - gills widely attached widely to stem

Adnexed - gills attached narrowly to stem

Decurrent - gills running down stem for some length

Emarginate - gills notched immediately before attaching to stem

Free - gills not attached to stem

Seceding - gills attached, but breaking away from stem at margin (often older specimens)

Sinuate - gills smoothly notched and running briefly down stem

Subdecurrent - gills running briefly down stem

Cap morphology

Campanulate - bell-shaped

Conical - triangular

Convex - outwardly rounded

Depressed - with a low central region

Flat - with top of uniform height

Infundibuliform - deeply depressed, funnel-shaped

Ovate - shaped like half an egg

Umbillicate - with a small, deep depression

Umbonate - with a central bump or knob

Mushroom cap morphology.[49]

Techniques for Safe Identification

- **Observe Meticulously:** Examine all parts of the mushroom closely, including the cap (color, shape, texture, presence of a veil), gills (color, spacing, attachment style), stipe (length, thickness, texture, presence of a ring or bulb), and any other distinguishing features. Some mushrooms lack certain features, so a comprehensive evaluation is crucial.

- **Spore Print Magic:** This technique is a powerful identification tool. Take a mature mushroom cap, place it gill-side down on a clean sheet of paper, and cover it with a glass or bowl. Leave it undisturbed for a few hours. The spores will fall onto the paper, creating a spore print. The color and shape of the spore print are essential clues for identification. Consult your field guides to match the spore print with specific species descriptions.

- **Habitat Matters:** Different mushroom species favor specific habitats. Learn about the types of trees, soil conditions, and elevations where your target edible species typically grows. Observing the surrounding environment can be a valuable piece of the identification puzzle. For example, chanterelles often grow in association with oak trees, while morels prefer disturbed areas.

- **Never Rely on a Single Feature:** Mushrooms can vary in color, size, and even shape depending on age and growing conditions. Don't rely solely on one characteristic for identification. Always consider a combination of factors, including cap shape, gill structure, stipe features, spore print color, and habitat.

- **When in Doubt, Leave It Out:** This golden rule cannot be emphasized enough. If you have even the slightest uncertainty about a mushroom's identity, err on the side of caution and leave it behind. There will always be another opportunity to forage, and your health is not worth the risk.

The Power of Verification

Once you've narrowed down your identification to a few possible species, verify your findings with multiple sources. Here's a multi-step verification approach:

1. Compare your observations with detailed descriptions and high-quality photographs in your field guides.
2. Consult online resources from trusted websites and mycological societies.
3. Share clear photographs and detailed notes with experienced mushroom foragers or a local mycological society for verification.

Mushroom identification is a continuous learning process. The more you practice, observe, and consult, the more confident you'll become in distinguishing edible from inedible and poisonous species.

Safety Considerations

The thrill of discovering a hidden patch of mushrooms can be intoxicating, but the excitement must be tempered with a healthy dose of caution. While a rewarding pursuit, mushroom foraging demands a deep respect for the delicate balance of the natural world and a commitment to safe practices. Here, you explore crucial safety considerations and techniques to ensure a sustainable and enjoyable experience.

The Necessity of Accurate Identification

The cornerstone of safe mushroom foraging is accurate identification. As tempting as it may be to harvest a basketful of beautiful mushrooms, even a single mistake can have serious consequences. Some mushrooms bear an uncanny resemblance to their edible counterparts yet are highly toxic, causing everything from mild stomach upset to liver failure and even death. Never consume a wild mushroom unless you can identify it with absolute certainty.

Beware of Toxic Look-Alikes

Nature can be a master of deception. Many edible mushrooms have poisonous look-alikes that share similar characteristics. Here are some common examples to illustrate the dangers:

- Chanterelles: (safe and delicious) can be mistaken for Jack-o'-Lanterns (highly toxic and can cause hallucinations). Look for the false gills and the absence of true gills (instead, Jack-o'-Lanterns have pores) on the underside of the cap.

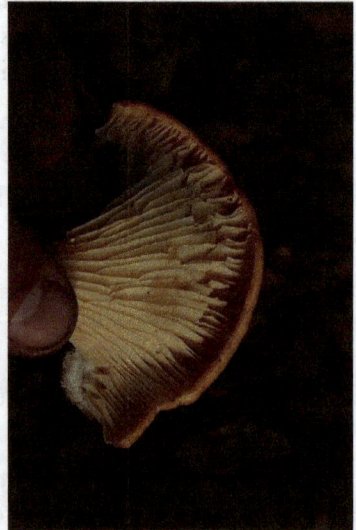

This is a toxic Jack-o'-Lantern mushroom (*Omphalotus olearius*; don't mistake it for a Chanterelle.[50]

- **Morels:** These prized edibles are often confused with their cousins in the genus *Gyromitra*, or false morels. Although one species (*G. esculenta*) is still commonly eaten, most if not all false morels are toxic, and should be avoided. False morels have a brain-like wrinkled cap, unlike the true morel's pitted or honeycomb-like cap.

Always Prioritize Safety: When in doubt, leave it out. This may seem disappointing, but it's a far better option than risking serious illness. There will always be another opportunity to forage, and a healthy respect for the power of wild mushrooms is paramount.

By prioritizing safety, practicing responsible harvesting techniques, and fostering a deep respect for the natural world, you can ensure that mushroom foraging remains a sustainable and rewarding activity for generations to come. The thrill of the hunt is best enjoyed with a healthy dose of caution and a commitment to protecting the ecosystem's delicate balance.

Profiles of Common Edible Mushrooms

The Northeast boasts a diverse array of edible mushrooms, each with its own unique flavor and culinary applications. This section delves into the profiles of some commonly found and easily identifiable species, empowering you to embark on a safe and rewarding foraging adventure. Prioritize safety and accurate identification above all else. If you are unsure about a mushroom's identity, leave it behind.

Chanterelle (*Cantharellus* spp.)

The chanterelle, with its golden yellow, trumpet-shaped cap and distinctive forked gills, is a prized edible mushroom sought after by foragers worldwide. Its fruity, apricot-like aroma and peppery flavor add a touch of magic to various dishes.

Chanterelle.[51]

Distinct Characteristics

- **Cap:** Trumpet- or funnel-shaped, often with wavy or lobed edges. Color ranges from bright yellow to orange-yellow.

- **Gills:** Chanterelles have false "gills" that are actually just folds in the underside of the cap. They are blunt, forked, and extend down the stem.

- **Stipe:** Cylindrical, smooth, generally lateral (off-center) and the same color as the cap.

- **Spore Print:** Creamy white to pale yellow.

Preferred Habitats: Chanterelles form mycorrhizal relationships with both hardwoods and conifers, including oaks, beeches, pines, and birches. Look for them on the forest floor beneath these host trees, particularly on acidic, well-drained soils. They are most abundant in the summer and early fall.

Seasonal Nuances: The prime season for chanterelles is from late summer to early fall, although this can vary depending on weather conditions.

Nutritional Benefits: Chanterelles are a good source of vitamins A, C, and D. They also contain fiber, potassium, and some B vitamins.

Accurate Identification: Look for the vibrant yellow caps and forked gills, which should be similar in color to the caps. If unsure, take a spore print: if it's a true chanterelle, it will be white or pale yellow. Avoid chanterelle look-alikes with true gills or a different spore print color.

Potential Look-Alikes: Jack-o'-Lantern mushrooms (*Omphalotus olearius*) can look like chanterelles due to their orange caps, they have true gills that do not fork and a white-to-orange spore print. Additionally, Jack-o'-Lanterns often glow faintly in the dark, a characteristic not shared by chanterelles.

Fun Fact: Chanterelles contain a compound that repels insects and other pests. This is why they are often found in good condition, even after reaching maturity.

Oyster Mushroom (*Pleurotus ostreatus*)

The oyster mushroom is a popular and versatile edible fungus, so named for its resemblance to the shellfish. These fan- or spoon-shaped mushrooms have soft, grayish-white caps and are easily identifiable, even by beginners.

Oyster mushroom.[53]

Distinct Characteristics

- **Cap:** Fan-shaped or spoon-shaped, with smooth, often glossy caps that may be brown, grayish, white, or even blue. The cap edges often become upturned, wavy, or lobed as they age.
- **Gills:** White or cream-colored, thin, and closely spaced. They extend partially down the length of the stem.
- **Stipe:** Short, lateral (growing off-center from the cap), and often attached to the substrate (the surface where it grows) with a fuzzy base.
- **Spore Print:** White to lilac-white.

Preferred Habitats: Oyster mushrooms grow on decaying hardwood logs, stumps, and branches. Look for them in clusters on trees in various stages of decomposition, particularly in moist, shaded areas. They can be found throughout the year, but fruiting is most prolific in the spring and fall.

Seasonal Nuances: The ideal time to find oyster mushrooms is in the spring and fall, especially after a rain.

Nutritional Benefits: Oyster mushrooms are a good source of protein, fiber, vitamins B and D, and essential minerals like potassium and phosphorus.

Accurate Identification: Look for the fan-shaped cap, gills that run down the stem, and the white to lilac-white spore print.

Potential Look-Alikes: Angel Wings (*Pleurocybella porrecta*) can resemble oyster mushrooms, but has thinner and tougher flesh and grows on conifer trees, especially hemlocks (*Tsuga* spp.). Although once considered edible, it has come to be regarded as potentially toxic and should be avoided.

Fun Fact: Oyster mushrooms are one of the few that can be easily cultivated at home. You can purchase mushroom growing kits to grow your fresh oyster mushrooms all year round.

Hen-of-the-Woods (*Grifola frondosa*)

The Hen-of-the-Woods mushroom, also known as *maitake* or "dancing mushroom," is a prized edible fungus with a particular appearance and a delicate, complex flavor. These large, feathery clusters of grayish-brown caps cascading down the stipe resemble a hen's ruffled feathers, making them a captivating find for foragers.

Dancing mushrooms.[53]

Distinct Characteristics

- **Cap:** Numerous dark grayish-brown to light brown caps are often overlapping and clustered in a rosette. The caps can be lobed, wavy, or fan-shaped with a slightly scaly texture.
- **Underside:** Creamy white to light brown angular pores, approximately 2-3 per millimeter. Pores run down the length of the stem nearly to the base.

- **Stipe:** Black at the base, gradually lightening to brown towards the top. The stipe is often thick and fleshy, with a rough or hairy texture.
- **Spore Print:** White to creamy white.

Preferred Habitats: Hen-of-the-Woods mushrooms are saprobic (living on dead wood) on hardwoods, especially oaks, and sometimes weakly parasitic. They generally emerge at the bases of trees, often in the same place for several years, throughout summer and fall.

Seasonal Nuances: The prime season for Hen-of-the-Woods mushrooms is from late August to early November.

Nutritional Benefits: Hen-of-the-Woods mushrooms are a powerhouse of nutrients. They are rich in vitamins B and C, contain minerals like potassium and magnesium, and are a good source of dietary fiber. Additionally, Hen-of-the-Woods mushrooms have been linked to potential health benefits, including boosting the immune system and fighting inflammation. (Note: More research is needed to confirm these possible benefits.)

Accurate Identification: The combination of the numerous, overlapping grayish-brown caps cascading down a thick, black-based stipe is a key identifier. Look for the white to creamy white spore print for confirmation. Avoid any look-alikes with different cap colors, spore print colors, or a smooth stipe.

Potential Look-Alikes: Although hen-of-the-woods has no toxic or dangerous lookalikes, a few other polypores (shelf fungi) can appear similar. The closest in appearance is the black-staining polypore (*Meripilus sumstinei*), which also forms rosettes of overlapping caps at the bases of oaks. However, true to its name this mushroom has flesh that turns black when bruised or broken.

Fun Fact: The name "Dancing Mushroom" originates from a legend in Japan, where Hen-of-the-Woods mushrooms were believed to be so delicious that people would dance with joy after finding them.

This chapter has unveiled a glimpse into the fascinating Northeast mushrooms. You've explored the ecological significance of fungi, delved into basic mushroom anatomy for safe identification, and equipped yourself with essential tips and techniques for responsible foraging. You've also explored the profiles of some common and delicious edible mushrooms, piquing your curiosity and encouraging you to investigate further.

Mushroom identification is a lifelong pursuit. Always prioritize safety, consult multiple resources, and only consume a wild mushroom if you are 100% certain of its identity. Embrace the learning process, join a local mycological society, and embark on a rewarding adventure into the hidden kingdom of Northeast mushrooms. The forest awaits, teeming with diverse fungal treasures waiting to be discovered.

Chapter 6: Cooking Wild Edibles: Delicious and Easy Recipes

The thrill of foraging doesn't end with the discovery of your wild edibles. This chapter transforms your foraged loot into culinary delights. You'll discover simple and delicious recipes that showcase the flavors of wild greens, vibrant flowers, juicy berries, and earthy roots. You'll also explore delectable ways to prepare the mushrooms you've identified, unlocking their full potential in a variety of dishes.

Whether you're a seasoned forager or a curious newcomer, this chapter offers something for every palate and skill level. You'll find basic preparations for different types of wild edibles, ensuring you get the most out of your harvest. Get ready to transform your wild bounty into

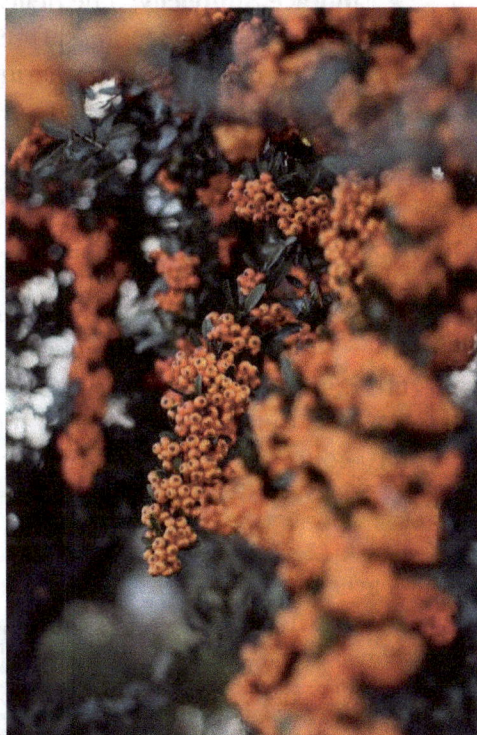

Wild red berries.[54]

97

unforgettable dishes, adding a touch of nature to your table. However, before you dive into specific dishes, equip yourself with some essential cooking tips for wild edibles:

- **Freshness Is Key:** As with any ingredient, freshness is vital for wild edibles. Eat your foraged treasures soon after harvest for the best flavor and texture.

- **Start Small:** If you're new to wild edibles, begin by adding them to familiar dishes in small quantities. This allows you to gradually become accustomed to their flavors and textures.

- **Proper Cleaning:** Always clean your foraged finds thoroughly before cooking. Rinse them gently in cool water, removing any dirt, debris, or insects. Some plants may require additional steps, such as blanching or soaking, to remove bitterness or potential toxins. Consult your field guides or reliable online resources for specific cleaning instructions for different wild edibles.

- **Embrace Simplicity:** The delicate flavors of wild ingredients often shine brightest in unfussy preparations. Simple techniques like sautéing, roasting, or simmering allow the natural essence of your foraged finds to take center stage.

- **Experiment and Explore:** Use these recipes as a springboard for your culinary creativity. Combine wild ingredients, explore different flavor profiles, and discover the endless possibilities that nature's bounty offers.

With these tips in mind, get ready to explore recipes for a variety of wild edibles, from salads bursting with fresh greens and flowers to hearty soups brimming with earthy roots and tubers. Prepare to unveil delectable ways to cook the mushrooms you've meticulously identified, transforming them into mouthwatering appetizers, main courses, and even side dishes.

Creamy Chanterelle Risotto

As the leaves blaze with fiery hues and the air crisps with a hint of winter's breath, there's nothing quite as comforting as a warm bowl of risotto. This recipe elevates the classic dish to new heights by incorporating the flavor of chanterelle mushrooms. Earthy, subtly fruity, and boasting a beautiful golden hue, chanterelles weave their magic into every creamy bite. Gather your harvest, invite your loved ones, and prepare to savor the essence of autumn with this delectable Chanterelle Risotto.

Ingredients:

- 4 cups vegetable broth, warmed
- 2 tablespoons unsalted butter
- 1 tablespoon olive oil
- 1 finely chopped shallot
- 1 cup Arborio rice
- 1/2 cup dry white wine
- 1/2 cup grated Parmesan cheese, plus extra for serving
- 1 teaspoon fresh thyme leaves, chopped (or 1/2 teaspoon dried thyme)
- Salt and freshly ground black pepper to taste
- 12 ounces fresh chanterelle mushrooms, cleaned and sliced
- 1/4 cup chopped fresh parsley

Instructions:

1. **Making the Broth:** Heat up the vegetables in a saucepan; a medium-sized one would be great. Do this over medium heat and let it simmer as you prepare the rest.

2. **Sautéing the Aromatics:** Put the butter and olive oil in a Dutch oven or a big heavy bottom pot. Melt over medium heat, and then put in the shallots. Stir gently until they are translucent and soft. This can take around 3 minutes.

3. **Toasting the Rice:** To the same pot as the aromatics, put in the rice and stir continuously for around a minute. You'll know that it's toasted when the color changes slightly and becomes translucent.

4. **Deglazing with Wine:** Add the wine and let it simmer while stirring every now and then until it is almost fully absorbed.

5. **Gradually Adding the Broth:** Add the broth half a cup at a time. Make sure that you continuously stir to let the rice absorb the liquid before adding the next batch. Keep doing this until the rice cooks enough to just have a slight bite to it. This should take around 20 minutes. The total amount of broth used may vary depending on your rice.

6. **Incorporating the Chanterelles:** You can add the mushrooms as the last batch of broth is added. Make sure you continue to stir for 5 mins.

7. **Final Touches:** Stir in the pepper, salt, thyme, and Parmesan. Taste and adjust seasonings as needed.

8. **Serve and Enjoy:** Garnish with fresh parsley and serve immediately with extra Parmesan cheese on the side. Savor the creamy texture, the earthy depth of the chanterelles, and the comforting warmth of this autumnal delight.

Nettle and Potato Soup

Beyond the manicured lawns and cultivated gardens lie hidden edible treasures. Stinging nettles, often dismissed as pesky weeds, hold a surprising secret. This recipe transforms nettles from garden foe to culinary hero, weaving them into a soul-warming soup alongside creamy potatoes and a touch of garlic. Earthy, slightly vegetal, and bursting with hidden vitamins, nettles add a unique twist to this comforting classic. Prepare to be delighted by this simple yet flavorful Nettle and Potato Soup.

Ingredients:

- 1 tablespoon olive oil
- 1 onion, chopped
- 2 cloves garlic, minced
- 4 cups vegetable broth
- 4 medium potatoes, peeled and diced
- 4 cups packed fresh nettles, blanched and chopped (or 2 cups frozen chopped nettles, thawed and squeezed dry)
- 1/2 cup heavy cream (optional)
- Salt and freshly ground black pepper to taste
- Fresh dill or chives, chopped (for garnish)

Instructions:

1. **Sauté the Aromatics:** Heat the olive oil over medium heat in a large pot or Dutch oven. Add the chopped onion and cook, stirring occasionally, until softened and translucent, about 5 minutes. Stir in the minced garlic and cook for an additional minute until fragrant.

2. **Broth and Potatoes:** Pour in the vegetable broth and bring to a boil. Add the diced potatoes and reduce heat to simmer. Cook for 15-20 minutes or until the potatoes are tender.

3. **Incorporate the Nettles:** Prepare the nettles while the potatoes are simmering. If using fresh nettles, wear gloves to protect your hands from stings. Blanch the nettles in boiling water for 30 seconds, then immediately transfer them to an ice bath to stop the cooking process. Drain the nettles well and chop them. Add the chopped nettles to the pot with the potatoes and broth.

4. **Creamy Enrichment (Optional):** If desired, stir in the heavy cream for a richer texture. Season the soup with salt and freshly ground black pepper to taste.

5. **Simmer and Serve:** Simmer the soup for an additional 5 minutes to allow the flavors to meld.

6. **Garnish and Enjoy:** Ladle the hot soup into bowls and garnish with chopped fresh dill or chives. Embrace the unique flavor of nettles and savor this nourishing and delicious creation.

Nettle and Potato Soup is simple, healthy, and surprisingly flavorful. This recipe offers a glimpse into the world beyond cultivated gardens. The next time you encounter a patch of nettles, don your gloves, embrace the wild, and create a taste of the untamed in your kitchen.

Dandelion and Chickweed Salad (or Wild Green Salad)

Spring unfolds a buffet of flavors, and nature's bounty extends far beyond cultivated gardens. This recipe celebrates the humble dandelion and chickweed, two often-overlooked "weeds" that transform into a delicious and nutritious salad. Dandelion greens are slightly bitter, while chickweed adds a touch of delicate earthiness. Together,

Dandelion and chickweed salad.[45]

they create a textural and flavor explosion, begging to be tossed with a simple vinaigrette.

Step outside, breathe in the fresh air and reconnect with nature's offerings. With a basket in hand and this recipe as your guide, you can create a delicious salad and a celebration of the wild world around us!

Ingredients (Feel free to adjust the proportions based on what you find)

- 4 cups dandelion greens (young tender leaves are best)
- 2 cups chickweed
- 1/2 cup thinly sliced red onion (optional)
- 1/4 cup crumbled feta cheese (optional)
- 1/4 cup toasted walnuts or pecans (optional)

Vinaigrette:

- 2 tablespoons olive oil
- 1 tablespoon lemon juice
- 1 tablespoon balsamic vinegar (or apple cider vinegar)
- 1 teaspoon Dijon mustard
- Salt and freshly ground black pepper to taste

Instructions:

1. **Prepare the Wild Greens:** Start by gathering your wild ingredients. If using dandelions, choose young, tender leaves, discarding any tough stems. Chickweed is used whole, including delicate flowers. Rinse the greens thoroughly in cool water to remove any dirt or debris. You can spin them dry in a salad spinner or pat them dry with a clean kitchen towel.

2. **Assemble the Salad:** In a large bowl, combine the dandelion greens, chickweed, and any additional ingredients you'd like to include, such as sliced red onion, crumbled feta cheese, or toasted nuts.

3. **Prepare the Vinaigrette:** In a small bowl, whisk together the olive oil, lemon juice, balsamic vinegar (or apple cider vinegar), and Dijon mustard. Season generously with salt and freshly ground black pepper.

4. **Dress and Serve:** Pour the vinaigrette over the salad and toss gently to coat all the ingredients. Taste and adjust seasonings as

needed.

5. **Savor the Wild:** Serve the Wild Green Salad immediately and savor the unique flavors of nature's bounty. This salad pairs well with grilled fish and roasted chicken, or it can be enjoyed on its own as a light and refreshing lunch.

This Dandelion and Chickweed Salad is a testament to the potential of exploring the wild edibles around us. Not only is it a delicious and healthy option, but it also fosters a connection with the natural world and a deeper appreciation for the simple yet remarkable flavors it offers. The next time you're out for a walk, keep an eye out for dandelions and chickweed because they might just become your new favorite salad ingredients.

Stuffed Wild Grape Leaves

Grapevines, with their cascading tendrils and jewel-toned fruit, are a familiar sight in many regions. However, beyond the juicy grapes lies another hidden gem: the leaves. Stuffed grape leaves are a culinary cornerstone of Mediterranean cuisine, wrapped in tradition and bursting with flavor. This recipe captures the essence of this dish, using readily available wild grape leaves and a simple yet flavorful vegetarian filling.

Stuffed grape leaves.[56]

Ingredients:

For the Grape Leaves:

- About 50 fresh wild grape leaves (washed and stems removed)
- 4 cups water
- 1/2 cup lemon juice

For the Stuffing:

- 1 cup long-grain white rice, rinsed
- 1/2 cup chopped onion
- 1/4 cup chopped fresh parsley
- 1/4 cup chopped fresh mint
- 2 tablespoons olive oil
- 1 tablespoon lemon juice
- 1 teaspoon dried oregano
- 1/2 teaspoon salt
- 1/4 teaspoon freshly ground black pepper

For Cooking:

- 1/2 cup olive oil
- 1 lemon, sliced

Instructions:

1. **Prepare the Grape Leaves:** Bring the water and lemon juice to a boil in a large pot. Add the grape leaves and simmer for 2-3 minutes or until they are wilted and pliable. Drain the leaves in a colander and rinse them with cool water. Carefully peel off any tough stems from the base of each leaf.

2. **Make the Stuffing:** In a large bowl, combine the rinsed rice, chopped onion, parsley, mint, olive oil, lemon juice, oregano, salt, and black pepper. Mix well to ensure all ingredients are evenly distributed.

3. **Assemble the Dolmas:** Lay a grape leaf flat on a work surface, vein side down. Place a small spoonful of the stuffing mixture near the base of the leaf. Fold the sides of the leaf inwards, then roll up tightly from the base to form a small cigar-shaped dolma. Repeat this with the remaining grape leaves and stuffing mixture.

4. **Simmer and Steam:** In a large pot with a tightly-fitting lid, arrange the dolmas in a single layer, seam side down. Pour the olive oil over the dolmas and add the lemon slices. Add enough water to barely cover the dolmas (about 1-2 cups). Bring to a boil, then reduce heat to low, cover the pot, and simmer gently for 45-50 minutes, or until the rice is cooked through and the grape leaves are tender.

5. **Cool and Serve:** Remove the pot from heat and let the dolmas cool slightly in the cooking liquid. Once cool enough to handle, transfer them to a serving platter. Stuffed grape leaves are traditionally served at room temperature or slightly chilled.

This recipe is a delightful introduction to the possibilities of stuffed grape leaves. With their stark green color, savory filling, and delicate texture, they are a true culinary adventure. Serve them as an appetizer, a side dish, or even a vegetarian main course. Enjoy the taste of the Mediterranean, all wrapped up in a bite-sized bundle of wild grape leaves.

Fiddlehead Fern and Bacon Quiche

Spring awakens the senses with vivid colors and fresh flavors. This Fiddlehead Fern and Bacon Quiche captures the essence of the season, weaving the delicate fiddleheads with savory bacon and creamy custard in a flaky pastry crust. Fiddleheads, with their interesting appearance and subtle earthiness, add a delightful textural and flavor contrast to the richness of the dish. This recipe is a celebration of the season, offering a delicious and satisfying brunch or light dinner option.

Ingredients:

For the Crust:

- 1 1/4 cups all-purpose flour
- 1/2 teaspoon salt
- 1/2 cup (1 stick) cold unsalted butter, cubed
- 3-4 tablespoons ice water

For the Filling:

- 8 slices thick-cut bacon, chopped
- 1 tablespoon olive oil
- 1 medium onion, chopped

- 1 1/2 cups fresh fiddlehead ferns, trimmed and cleaned
- 4 large eggs
- 1 1/2 cups milk
- 1/2 cup grated Parmesan cheese
- 1/4 teaspoon dried thyme
- Salt and freshly ground black pepper to taste

Instructions:

1. **Prepare the Crust:** Whisk together the flour and salt in a large bowl. Cut the cold butter into the flour mixture using a pastry cutter or your fingertips until it resembles coarse crumbs. Gradually add ice water, 1 tablespoon at a time, tossing with a fork until the dough just comes together. Be careful not to overmix. Form the dough into a disc, wrap it in plastic wrap, and refrigerate for at least 30 minutes.

2. **Preheat the Oven:** Preheat your oven to 375°F (190°C). Lightly grease a 9-inch pie dish.

3. **Roll Out the Dough:** Roll out the chilled dough to a 12-inch circle on a lightly floured surface. Carefully transfer the dough to the prepared pie dish and gently press it into the bottom and sides. Trim any excess dough from the edges. Crimp the edges decoratively, if desired. Pre-bake the crust for 10 minutes. Remove from the oven and let cool slightly.

4. **Cook the Bacon and Onions:** Heat the olive oil in a large skillet over medium heat while the crust is pre-baking. Add the chopped bacon and cook until crispy. Remove the bacon from the pan with a slotted spoon and set aside. Add the chopped onion to the remaining bacon fat in the pan and cook until softened and translucent, about 5 minutes.

5. **Prepare the Fiddleheads:** Bring a pot of salted water to a boil. Add the trimmed and cleaned fiddlehead ferns and cook for 3-5 minutes or until tender-crisp. Drain the fiddleheads and rinse with cold water to stop the cooking process.

6. **Whisk the Custard:** In a large bowl, whisk together the eggs, milk, Parmesan cheese, and dried thyme. Season with salt and freshly ground black pepper to taste.

7. **Assemble and Bake:** Scatter the cooked bacon and fiddleheads over the pre-baked crust. Pour the egg custard mixture over the top. Bake the quiche for 35-40 minutes until the custard is set and the crust is golden brown.

8. **Cool and Serve:** Remove the quiche from the oven and let it cool slightly on a wire rack before slicing and serving. Enjoy warm or at room temperature.

Fiddlehead Fern and Bacon Quiche is a delightful way to celebrate the flavors of spring. The delicate fiddleheads add a tasty touch, while the bacon and creamy custard provide a satisfying balance. Gather your ingredients, embrace the season, and bake this quiche for a memorable meal.

Wild Blueberry and Elderflower Jam

Summer's feast extends far beyond cultivated gardens. Wild blueberries, bursting with concentrated flavor, and elderflowers, with their delicate floral notes, combine to create a jam unlike any other. This recipe captures the essence of these seasonal treasures, transforming them into a flavorful spread that's perfect for toast, pastries, or simply savoring by the spoonful.

Gather your baskets and head out to explore the summer meadows. With a little effort and this easy recipe, you'll create a homemade jam that celebrates the wild flavors of the season.

Wild blueberry and elderflower jam.[57]

Ingredients:

- 4 cups fresh wild blueberries
- 1 1/2 cups granulated sugar
- 1/2 cup water

- 1/4 cup elderflower cordial (or 1 tablespoon dried elderflowers steeped in 1/4 cup hot water for 30 minutes, strained)
- 1 lemon, juiced
- 1 package (3 ounces) powdered fruit pectin

Instructions:

1. **Prepare the Berries:** Gently rinse the wild blueberries in a large bowl. Pick out any leaves or debris.

2. **Combine Fruit and Sugar:** In a large saucepan, combine the rinsed blueberries, granulated sugar, and water. Stir to combine and bring to a boil over medium heat.

3. **Elderflower Infusion:** Stir in the elderflower cordial (or strained elderflower tea) and lemon juice. Reduce heat to medium-low and simmer for 10-15 minutes, stirring occasionally, until the berries soften and the mixture begins to thicken.

4. **Activate the Pectin:** Whisk together the powdered fruit pectin with 2 tablespoons of sugar in a small bowl.

5. **Reaching the Set Point:** Increase the heat to medium-high and bring the jam mixture to a rolling boil. Once boiling, slowly whisk in the pectin mixture and continue boiling for 1 minute, stirring constantly.

6. **Foam Reduction (Optional):** If a significant amount of foam forms during the boiling process, you can skim it off with a spoon.

7. **Final Touches and Canning:** Remove the jam from the heat. For a clearer jam, you can skim off any remaining foam. Following proper canning procedures (consult a reliable canning resource for specific instructions), fill sterilized jars with the hot jam, leaving a small headspace at the top. Seal the jars according to canning guidelines.

Wild Blueberry and Elderflower Jam is an excellent example of the delicious possibilities of foraging. The stark color, the burst of blueberry flavor with a subtle hint of elderflower, and the homemade satisfaction make this jam a true summer treasure. Enjoy it on toast or biscuits, or simply savor its unique flavor with a spoonful. When foraging, prioritize safety and identify your wild ingredients with certainty.

Hen-of-the-Woods Tacos

Step aside, typical taco Tuesday. These Hen-of-the-Woods Tacos offer a symphony of textures and flavors, celebrating the unique qualities of this prized edible mushroom. Hen-of-the-Woods, also known as Maitake, boasts a meaty texture and a delicate, woodsy aroma. Paired with a simple marinade and nestled in warm tortillas, they create a vegetarian taco experience that's anything but ordinary.

Ingredients:

For the Marinated Mushrooms:

- 1 pound Hen-of-the-Woods mushrooms broken into bite-sized pieces
- 2 tablespoons olive oil
- 1 tablespoon soy sauce
- 1 tablespoon lime juice
- 1 teaspoon dried oregano
- 1/2 teaspoon smoked paprika
- 1/4 teaspoon garlic powder
- Salt and freshly ground black pepper to taste

For the Tacos:

- 8 corn tortillas, warmed
- 1 cup crumbled queso fresco (or feta cheese)
- 1/2 cup chopped red onion
- 1/4 cup chopped fresh cilantro
- Avocado slices (optional)
- Lime wedges

Instructions:

1. **Marinate the Mushrooms:** In a large bowl, combine the olive oil, soy sauce, lime juice, oregano, smoked paprika, garlic powder, salt, and pepper. Add the bite-sized Hen-of-the-Woods mushrooms and toss to coat them evenly in the marinade. Let the mushrooms marinate for at least 15 minutes or up to 30 minutes for deeper flavor.

2. **Cook the Mushrooms:** Heat a large skillet or grill pan over medium heat. Add the marinated mushrooms and cook for 5-7 minutes per side or until golden brown and tender.

3. **Assemble the Tacos:** Warm your corn tortillas according to package instructions or how you like them(griddle, stovetop, or microwave). Fill each tortilla with cooked Hen-of-the-Woods mushrooms, crumbled queso fresco (or feta cheese), chopped red onion, and fresh cilantro. Add avocado slices for an extra creamy touch (optional).

4. **Serve and Enjoy:** Squeeze fresh lime juice over the tacos for a burst of acidity. Serve immediately and savor the delicious vegetarian symphony in every bite.

Hen-of-the-Woods Tacos are a great example of the versatility and culinary potential of wild mushrooms. They offer a satisfying and flavorful vegetarian option, perfect for taco nights, casual gatherings, or simply a delightful exploration of the edible world. The next time you encounter Hen-of-the-Woods mushrooms, bring them home and create this unique and delicious taco experience.

Cremini and Leek Fritters with Lemon Dill Sauce

Enjoy the humble cremini mushroom and elevate it to new heights with these Cremini and Leek Fritters. These crispy fritters are bursting with flavor and texture, making them a delightful appetizer, light lunch, or side dish. Leeks add a subtle oniony touch, while the lemon dill sauce provides a refreshing counterpoint.

Ingredients:

For the Fritters:

- 1 pound cremini mushrooms, finely chopped
- 1 large leek, white and light green parts only, thinly sliced
- 1/2 cup all-purpose flour
- 1/4 cup grated Parmesan cheese
- 1 large egg, beaten
- 1/4 cup chopped fresh parsley
- 1 teaspoon dried thyme

- Salt and freshly ground black pepper to taste
- Vegetable oil for frying

For the Lemon Dill Sauce:
- 1/2 cup sour cream
- 1/4 cup mayonnaise
- 1 tablespoon lemon juice
- 1 tablespoon chopped fresh dill
- Salt and freshly ground black pepper to taste

Instructions:

1. **Prepare the Ingredients:** Finely chop the cremini mushrooms and thinly slice the leek's white and light green parts. In a large bowl, whisk together the flour and Parmesan cheese.

2. **Combine the Wet and Dry Ingredients:** In a separate bowl, whisk together the beaten egg, chopped parsley, and dried thyme. Season with salt and pepper. Gradually add the wet ingredients to the dry ingredients, mixing until just combined. Fold in the chopped mushrooms and leeks.

3. **Fry the Fritters:** Heat a generous amount of vegetable oil in a large skillet over medium heat. Once hot, drop tablespoons of the batter into the oil, flattening them slightly with the back of a spoon. Fry for 2-3 minutes per side or until golden brown and cooked through. Drain the fritters on paper towels to remove excess oil.

4. **Make the Sauce:** In a small bowl, whisk together the sour cream, mayonnaise, lemon juice, and chopped dill. Season with salt and pepper to taste.

5. **Serve and Enjoy:** Serve the hot Cremini and Leek Fritters with a generous dollop of lemon dill sauce on the side. These fritters are best enjoyed fresh out of the pan but can also be kept warm in a preheated oven for a short time.

Chanterelle and Asparagus Pasta with Goat Cheese

Spring unfolds a bouquet of fresh flavors, and this Chanterelle and Asparagus Pasta captures the essence of the season in a delightful dish. Earthy chanterelle mushrooms mingle with asparagus spears, all tossed in a creamy goat cheese sauce. The result is a symphony of textures and flavors that's perfect for a satisfying vegetarian meal.

Chanterelle and asparagus pasta with goat cheese.[58]

Ingredients:

- 1 pound asparagus, trimmed and cut into bite-sized pieces
- 8 ounces dried pasta (such as penne or tagliatelle)
- 4 tablespoons unsalted butter
- 1 shallot, finely chopped
- 12 ounces chanterelle mushrooms, cleaned and sliced
- 1/2 cup dry white wine
- 1 cup heavy cream
- 4 ounces goat cheese, crumbled
- 1/4 cup grated Parmesan cheese
- Salt and freshly ground black pepper to taste
- Fresh chopped parsley, for garnish (optional)

Instructions:

1. **Cook the Asparagus:** Bring a large pot of salted water to a boil. Add the asparagus spears and cook for 3-4 minutes or until tender-crisp. Drain the asparagus, reserving 1/4 cup of the cooking water, and set aside.

2. **Cook the Pasta:** Return the pot of salted water to a boil and cook the pasta according to package instructions. Drain the pasta, reserving about 1/2 cup of the pasta water.

3. **Sauté the Mushrooms:** While the pasta is cooking, melt the butter in a large skillet over medium heat. Add the chopped shallot and cook until softened and translucent, about 3 minutes. Stir in the sliced chanterelle mushrooms and cook for 5-7 minutes or until golden brown and tender.

4. **Deglaze with Wine:** Pour in the white wine and cook, scraping up any browned bits from the bottom of the pan until the liquid is almost entirely reduced.

5. **Create the Creamy Sauce:** Stir in the heavy cream and reserved pasta water. Bring to a simmer and cook for 2-3 minutes, until the sauce thickens slightly. Remove the pan from heat and stir in the crumbled goat cheese and grated Parmesan cheese. Season with salt and freshly ground black pepper to taste.

6. **Combine and Serve:** In a large bowl, toss the cooked pasta, cooked asparagus, and creamy mushroom sauce together. If the sauce seems too thick, add a splash or two of the reserved pasta water to thin it out. Garnish with fresh chopped parsley (optional) and serve immediately.

As the last rays of the setting sun cast long shadows across the kitchen counter, the aroma of sizzling mushrooms and creamy goat cheese sauce fills the air. A steaming bowl of Chanterelle and Asparagus Pasta with Goat Cheese sits before you, a testament to the bounty of the season captured in a single dish. Each bite is a symphony of textures and flavors, the earthy chanterelles dancing with the crisp asparagus, and all enveloped in a luxurious goat cheese sauce.

This Chanterelle and Asparagus Pasta with Goat Cheese is a celebration of spring flavors. The creamy goat cheese sauce perfectly complements the earthy mushrooms and asparagus, creating a delightful vegetarian meal. Enjoy it with a loaf of crusty bread to soak up the delicious sauce.

Your kitchen is a canvas tonight, and you, the artist, have created a masterpiece. Take a moment to savor this creation, a celebration of fresh ingredients and culinary exploration. Let the warmth of the dish and the satisfaction of a meal cooked with love nourish your body and soul. After all, the true magic lies in the final product, the journey of discovery, and the joy of creating something delicious from scratch. Now, with a contented sigh and a heart full of culinary accomplishment, turn the page and prepare for your next culinary adventure.

Chapter 7: Foraging and Using Medicinal Plants

Step beyond the cultivated garden and into the forest of wild edibles. The Northeast's rich tapestry of medicinal plants, each harboring properties that have been harnessed for centuries in traditional healing practices. This chapter explores the fascinating concept of herbalism, unveiling the secrets held within the roots, leaves, and flowers of native plants.

Important Disclaimer: Before embarking on your herbal adventure, it's crucial to prioritize safety and responsible foraging practices. Always consult with a qualified healthcare professional before using any plant for medicinal purposes. Self-diagnosis and self-medication are dangerous, and some plants can have harmful interactions with medications or existing health conditions. This

Herbs have plenty of healing properties.[59]

chapter is a guide to exploring the fascinating medicinal plants, but it is never a substitute for professional medical advice.

Now, with a spirit of exploration and a healthy dose of caution, prepare to discover the Northeast's hidden healers, unveil the wisdom of traditional herbalism, and learn how to incorporate these natural wonders into a holistic approach to well-being.

The Enduring Power of Herbal Medicine

The concept of using plants for healing stretches back millennia, weaving itself through the history of various cultures. Even today, plants continue to play a significant role in modern holistic health practices. It's time to uncover the fascinating history of herbal medicine, exploring its ancient roots and enduring relevance.

Ancient Wisdom

Here are some fascinating examples of how ancient cultures harnessed the power of plants.

- **Early Civilizations:** From ancient Sumeria to Egypt and China, civilizations documented the use of plants for medicinal purposes. Archaeological evidence and historical texts reveal knowledge of medicinal plants dating back thousands of years.

- **Traditional Knowledge:** Indigenous cultures worldwide have developed vast repositories of herbal knowledge passed down through generations. This wisdom forms the foundation of many traditional healing systems still practiced today.

- **Bridging the Gap:** Modern science is increasingly investigating the traditional uses of plants, validating their effectiveness, and identifying the active compounds responsible for their medicinal properties.

The knowledge of medicinal plants wasn't static; it evolved through trade, cultural exchange, and continuous experimentation. This brings you to the next chapter in the story of herbal medicine.

From Folk Remedy to Formalized Medicine

Following the decline of the Roman Empire, herbal medicine took a new shape in Europe. Here's how herbal knowledge was preserved and disseminated during this period.

- **Medieval Europe:** Following the decline of the Roman Empire, herbal medicine flourished in Europe. Monasteries became centers of herbal knowledge, cultivating medicinal plants and compiling vast herbal libraries.

- **Standardization and Documentation:** As scientific understanding grew, efforts were made to document and categorize medicinal plants. This led to the development of pharmacopeias and official lists of medicinal plants with their properties and uses.

- **The Rise of Modern Medicine:** With the rise of synthetic pharmaceuticals in the 20th century, the use of herbal remedies declined in Western medicine. However, interest in natural approaches to health never entirely disappeared.

The decline of herbal medicine in Western practices wasn't the end of the story. It paved the way for a resurgence in modern times.

Reintroducing Herbs in Modern Healthcare

In recent decades, there's been a shift towards a more holistic approach to health. Here are some factors contributing to the renewed interest in herbal remedies.

- **Growing Interest:** Recently, there's been a renewed interest in natural and holistic approaches to health. This has led to a growing appreciation for the potential benefits of herbal remedies.

- **Complementary and Alternative Medicine:** Many people are integrating herbal medicine with conventional treatments as part of a holistic approach to well-being. Herbal remedies can offer relief from symptoms, support overall health, and potentially reduce reliance on certain medications.

- **Scientific Validation:** Modern scientific research is increasingly exploring the efficacy of herbal remedies. While more research is needed, some herbs have shown promising results for various health conditions.

The renewed interest in herbal medicine highlights its potential to complement modern healthcare practices. However, it's necessary to understand the limitations of herbal remedies.

Safety and Responsible Use

Herbal medicine is a powerful tool, but it's crucial to use it responsibly. Here are some key considerations to ensure the safe and effective use of herbal remedies.

- **Not a Replacement:** Herbal remedies should not be seen as a replacement for conventional medical treatments. For severe health conditions, consulting a qualified healthcare professional is crucial.

- **Quality and Consistency:** The quality and consistency of herbal products can vary. Choosing reputable brands and discussing potential interactions with any medications you're taking is important.

- **Individualized Approach:** What works for one person may not work for another. It's essential to consider individual needs and sensitivities when exploring herbal remedies.

Herbal medicine is a powerful tool, but it has limitations. By using it responsibly and in conjunction with conventional medicine when necessary, you'll harness the power of plants to support your overall well-being.

A Guide to Native Medicinal Plants

The Northeast boasts diverse types of flora, and woven within this dynamic landscape lies a treasure of medicinal plants. Each species offers a unique combination of properties that have been harnessed for centuries by indigenous cultures and herbalists. This section unearths some fascinating botanical healers, exploring their characteristics, habitats, and potential benefits.

Chamomile (*Matricaria chamomilla*)

Chamomile, a member of the aster family, has long been valued for its calming properties. This delicate flowering herb has been used for centuries to relieve anxiety, indigestion, and inflammation.

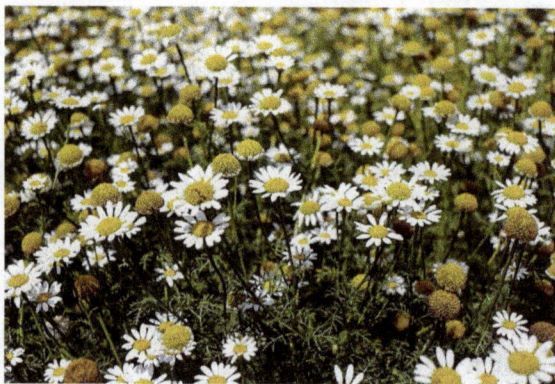

Chamomile.[60]

118

- **Distinct Characteristics:** Chamomile boasts feathery green leaves and daisy-like flowers with white petals and yellow centers. The flower heads have a strong, apple-like aroma.

- **Preferred Habitats:** Chamomile thrives in sunny, well-drained locations with sandy or loamy soil. It's often found in disturbed areas, wastelands, and along roadsides.

- **Seasonal Nuances:** Chamomile flowers bloom from late spring to early summer. Harvest the flower heads just as they open for the strongest potency.

- **Nutritional Benefits:** Chamomile contains numerous active compounds, including flavonoids, apigenin, and volatile oils. These compounds are believed to contribute to its calming and anti-inflammatory properties.

- **Accurate Identification:** Look for the finely divided leaves and daisy-like flower heads, which are about an inch in diameter with bulging, dome-like centers. The leaves and single flower heads with white ray florets surrounding a yellow disc center.

- **Potential Look-Alikes or Poisonous Counterparts:** Mayweed (*Matricaria discoidea*) is closely related to chamomile and is similar in appearance, but it can easily be distinguished by its flower heads, which lack ray florets and smell strongly of pineapple (it's also commonly called *pineappleweed*).

Lemon Balm (*Melissa officinalis*)

Lemon balm, a member of the mint family, is a fragrant herb known for its uplifting and calming properties. It's traditionally used to ease anxiety, promote sleep, and soothe digestive issues.

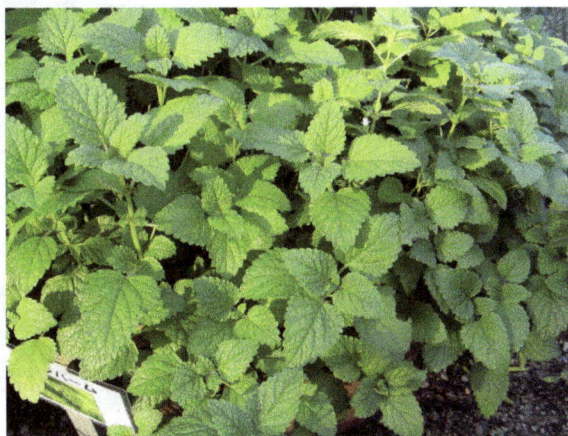

Lemon balm.[61]

- **Distinct Characteristics:** Lemon balm has wrinkly, oval leaves with scalloped edges, which like all plants in the mint family are arranged in opposite pairs on the stem. The leaves look a lot like mint leaves, but give off a refreshing lemon scent when crushed.

- **Preferred Habitats:** Lemon balm thrives in sunny locations with well-drained soil. It's often cultivated in herb gardens but has naturalized throughout the Northeast, in roadsides, pastures and meadows, and other sunny, disturbed areas.

- **Seasonal Nuances:** Lemon balm leaves can be harvested throughout the growing season, but they lose potency after the plants bolt.

- **Nutritional Benefits:** Lemon balm contains volatile oils, including citral and linalool, which are believed to contribute to its calming and mood-lifting properties.

- **Accurate Identification:** Lemon balm is distinguished from other members of the mint family by its lemon scent and the lack of hairy stems.

- **Potential Look-Alikes or Poisonous Counterparts:** Lemon balm has no close poisonous look-alikes. No species in the mint family is known to be toxic, although some people have reported allergic reactions.

Echinacea (*Echinacea purpurea*)

Introduction: Echinacea is a close relative of sunflowers (*Helianthus* spp.) and coneflowers (*Rudbeckia* spp.), and has long been valued for its immune-boosting properties. It's traditionally used to shorten the duration and severity of colds and flu.

Echinacea.[69]

- **Distinct Characteristics:** Echinacea features large compound flowers with pink or purple ray florets and a prominent orange cone in the center, which is slightly prickly to the touch. The leaves are lance-shaped with long stems, and all parts of the plant besides the flowers are hairy.

- **Preferred Habitats:** Echinacea prefers open areas like prairies, open woods, and even stream banks. – not to mention garden beds, as it's a popular ornamental plant.

- **Seasonal Nuances:** Echinacea flowers typically bloom from mid-summer to fall. Harvest the roots and leaves in the fall after the growing season ends for medicinal use.

- **Nutritional Benefits:** Echinacea contains various compounds, including alkylamides and cichoric acid, which are believed to stimulate the immune system.

- **Accurate Identification:** Echinacea's large pink-and-orange flowers are eye-catching and nearly unmistakable; after the "petals" drop off, the bristly cone-shaped centers remain, often persisting all winter long

- **Potential Look-alikes or Poisonous Counterparts:** Although a number of species of *Echinacea* are native to North America, only one is widespread and common, narrowleaved echinacea (*E. angustifolia*). Its thin leaves are fairly easy to distinguish, but both species can be used in medicine, for the same purposes.

Elderberry (*Sambucus nigra*)

Elder is a fast-growing and sometimes aggressive shrub, revered in Europe for the diverse medicinal uses of its dark purple berries, which are toxic when raw: thorough cooking degrades the toxic chemicals and improves the flavor of the berries, which are just as popular for the flavor as their health benefits.

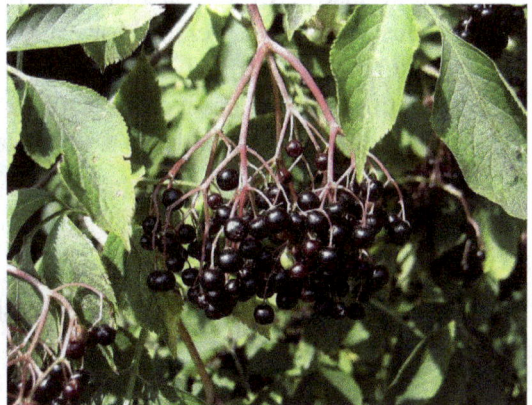

Sambucus Nigra.[68]

- **Distinct Characteristics:** Elders are slender, multi-trunked shrubs or small trees, often spreading via root sprouts and forming dense thickets. These produce showy, flat-topped clusters of white flowers in the spring, which mature into bunches of small, glossy purple berries in late summer and fall. The leaves are pinnate with serrated edges.

- **Preferred Habitats:** Elderberry thrives in moist, sunny locations especially along fencerows, forest edges, roadsides and waterways.

- **Seasonal Nuances:** The flowers bloom in late spring, and the berries ripen in late summer to early fall. However, only ripe, fully black berries are safe for consumption, and they must be cooked before consuming.

- **Nutritional Benefits:** Elderberries are rich in antioxidants, including anthocyanins, which are believed to contribute to their immune-supporting properties.

- **Accurate Identification:** It's crucial to accurately identify elderberry, as some parts of the elderberry plant, particularly the leaves and stems, are toxic if eaten raw. Look for the flat white flower clusters followed by dark purple berries.

- **Potential Look-Alikes or Poisonous Counterparts:** Mountain ash (*Sorbus americana*) can appear similar to elder as it has similar leaves, growth habit , and flowers. However, mountain ash leaves have many more leaflets (11-17), and these are not serrated, The toxic water hemlock (*Cicuta* spp.) has similar compound leaves and also grows near water – it even produces similar white clusters of flowers. However, water hemlock's leaves are alternately arranged, while elder leaves are oppositely paired, and hemlock is a herbaceous plant -- dying back to the ground each winter – whereas elder is a shrub or tree.

This brief exploration has unveiled just a taste of the Northeast's wealth of medicinal plants. Here are three more examples to pique your curiosity:

- **Goldenseal (Hydrastis canadensis):** This woodland perennial is known for its bright yellow root, which is traditionally used to support digestive health and fight infections. However, due to overharvesting, goldenseal is now considered a threatened species and should be ethically sourced if used at all.

- **Peppermint (Mentha piperita):** This aromatic herb is a familiar favorite, but its medicinal properties extend beyond freshening breath. Peppermint is traditionally used to soothe digestive discomfort, ease nausea, and improve respiratory function.
- **Yarrow (Achillea millefolium):** This common wildflower with flat, white flower clusters has been used for centuries for its wound-healing and anti-inflammatory properties. Yarrow is used topically as a poultice or wash for minor cuts and scrapes.

You've now explored a fascinating array of medicinal plants native to the Northeast.

Remember: This information is for educational purposes only and should not be a substitute for professional medical advice. Always consult with a qualified healthcare professional before using any plant for medicinal purposes.

Incorporating Herbal Remedies into Daily Life

You've ethically harvested your plant material from the Northeast's bounty, and now it's time to unlock its potential. Here are some basic methods for preparing and incorporating these medicinal plants into your daily routine, alongside some suggestions specific to the Northeast region:

Simple and Soothing Teas:

This is a simple and versatile method of extracting the therapeutic properties of herbs. Steep dried plant parts in hot water for a soothing and flavorful tea.

- **Brew a Northeast Classic:** Make a calming cup of chamomile tea to ease anxiety or sip on a cup of echinacea tea for immune support (both common finds in the Northeast.)
- **Seasonal Solutions:** During allergy season, brew a nettle tea (harvested responsibly in early spring or fall) to combat symptoms, or enjoy a cup of red clover tea (avoid if pregnant) for a natural source of phytoestrogens.

Tinctures for Targeted Relief:

For a concentrated herbal extract, prepare tinctures by soaking plant material in alcohol for an extended period. Tinctures are typically taken in droppers. Here are some Northeast-inspired ideas:

- **Joint Support:** Prepare a dandelion root tincture (avoid if taking blood thinners) to support healthy joints.

- **Digestive Aid:** Use a goldenseal tincture (use sparingly and consult a healthcare professional before use) to soothe occasional stomach upset.

Infused Oils for Topical Relief:

Harness the fat-soluble properties of plants by creating infused oils. Steep dried herbs in carrier oils like olive oil or jojoba oil for a potent topical remedy.

- **Soothing Skin:** Infuse calendula flowers (known for their skin-soothing properties) in a carrier oil, like sweet almond oil, to create a calming salve for irritated skin.

- **Muscle Relief:** Steep St. John's wort (consult a healthcare professional before use) in an oil like grapeseed oil to create a massage oil for sore muscles (avoid sun exposure after application).

Poultices for Targeted Relief

For localized pain relief or wound healing, poultices can be created by mashing fresh plant material and applying it directly to the affected area. Poultices made from mashed jewelweed (consult a herbalist for proper use) can offer quick relief for poison ivy rashes, a common Northeast summer woe.

How to Make a Poultice:

1. Wash and chop or grind your chosen herbs.
2. Moisten the plant material with hot water to create a thick paste.
3. Spread the paste on a clean cloth and apply directly to the affected area.
4. Secure the poultice with a bandage or gauze and leave it on for 20-30 minutes. Repeat as needed.

Salves for Long-lasting Comfort

Combine infused oils with beeswax and other ingredients to create soothing salves for irritated skin or minor cuts and scrapes.

How to Make a Salve:

1. In a double boiler, gently melt beeswax or another natural wax (like candelilla wax).

2.Add your infused oil and any other desired ingredients (like essential oils for fragrance).

3.Mix well and pour the liquid salve into tins or jars. Let it cool completely before using.

Tip: When using essential oils, always dilute them properly with a carrier oil before applying them topically.

Remember:

- Always research and identify plants correctly. Misidentification can be dangerous.
- Start with low doses and monitor your body's response.
- Consult a healthcare professional before using herbal remedies, especially if pregnant, breastfeeding, or taking medications.

The Northeast's wild medicinal plants have tremendous potential benefits; still, it's your responsibility to harvest them with respect and ensure their continued abundance for generations to come.

Essential Considerations for Using Medicinal Plants

The natural world offers a wide range of potential remedies, but venturing into the realm of herbal medicine requires a healthy dose of caution. This section sheds light on the safety considerations and potential risks associated with using medicinal plants, empowering you to make informed choices on your path to herbal wellness.

Allergies

Just like with any substance, allergic reactions can occur when using medicinal plants. Here's how to minimize the risk:

- **Start Low, Go Slow:** When trying a new herb, begin with a minimal dose and observe your body's response for at least 24 hours before increasing the amount.
- **Discontinue If Needed:** If you experience any adverse reactions, such as itching, rash, nausea, or dizziness, discontinue use immediately and consult a healthcare professional.
- **Know Your Allergies:** If you have any known allergies to plants or pollen, be cautious when trying new herbs. Research potential cross-reactions before using any medicinal plant.

Symptoms of
Allergic Rhinitis

- Stuffy itchy nose
- Sneezing
- Itchy
- Watery eyes

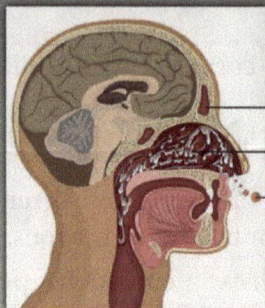

Swollen
sinuses

Mucus

Allergen

If you have a pollen allergy, then you might struggle with allergic rhinitis."

The Interplay with Medications

Some medicinal plants can interact with conventional medications, potentially reducing their effectiveness or causing unwanted side effects. Here's what to keep in mind:

- **Consult Your Doctor:** Before using any herbal remedy, discuss it with your doctor, especially if you take prescription medications, to prevent any dangerous interactions.

- **Be Transparent:** Disclose all herbal remedies you're using to your doctor, including the dosage and frequency. This ensures a holistic view of your health and medication regimen.

- **Exercise Caution:** Certain herbs like St. John's Wort can interact with antidepressants and other medications. Always research potential interactions before using any herb.

Finding the Right Dose

Dosage plays a crucial role in the safety and effectiveness of herbal remedies. Here are some pointers:

- **Start with a Low Dose:** As mentioned earlier, begin with a minimal dose and gradually increase as needed. This allows your body to adjust and minimizes the risk of side effects.

- **Respect the Plant's Power:** Don't assume that "more is better." Many herbs are potent, even in small quantities. Follow recommended dosages from reputable sources.

Consider Individual Factors: Dosage can vary based on factors like age, weight, and overall health. It's essential to consider these factors when using medicinal plants.

A Lifelong Journey of Learning

The usage of herbal medicine is ever-evolving. Here's how to cultivate a safe and enriching experience on your herbal journey:

- **Seek Reliable Sources:** Rely on reputable herbal references, websites, and qualified herbalists for accurate information on plant properties and safe use.

- **Continue Your Education:** Take advantage of workshops, online courses, and books to deepen your understanding of medicinal plants and their applications.

- **Practice Makes Perfect:** As you gain experience, experiment with different herbs and preparation methods, but always prioritize safety and responsible use.

Using medicinal plants requires ongoing learning and respect for the power of nature. By approaching herbalism with caution and a commitment to continuous education, you'll unlock its potential for holistic well-being while mitigating potential risks. This chapter has provided a foundational understanding of responsible foraging, preparation methods, and safety considerations.

Chapter 8: Embracing a Foraging Lifestyle

As you turn the final page of this chapter, take a moment to reflect on the journey you've undertaken. A transformation has unfolded from the initial spark of curiosity about the wild edibles gracing your local landscape to the newfound confidence in identifying and harvesting these botanical treasures. This exploration wasn't merely about acquiring knowledge or filling your basket with wild bounty. It was a deeper awakening, a reconnection with the

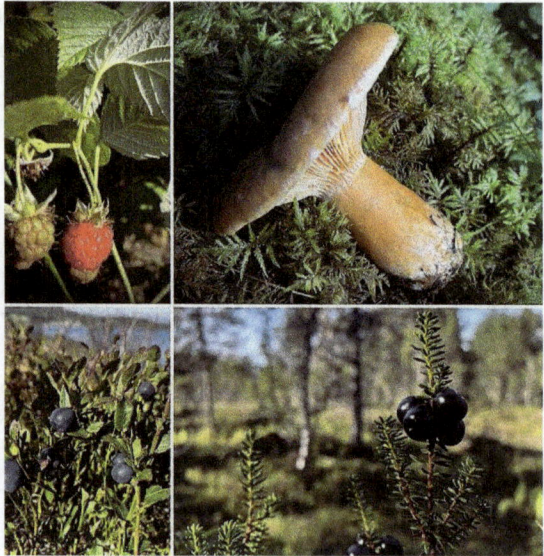

Foraging allows you to explore nature and bask in its beauty.[65]

rhythm of nature and the simple joy of living in harmony with the natural world.

This concluding chapter celebrates the art of embracing a foraging lifestyle. It's not just about the thrill of the hunt or the satisfaction of preparing a delicious meal with homegrown ingredients. It's about cultivating a deeper appreciation for the ecosystem's delicate balance, increasing self-reliance, and integrating the wisdom of traditional practices into your daily life.

Harmony with the Natural Cycle

The journey of a forager is a dance with the seasons. Throughout this book, you've learned to identify and appreciate the ever-changing bounty of the Northeast landscape. Now, it's time to dive deeper into the joys of living in harmony with this natural cycle.

- **Spring's Awakening:** Spring bursts forth with an abundance of tender greens like dandelion greens and nettles, perfect for adding a vivid touch to salads or stir-fries. Early blooming wildflowers, such as violets and dandelions, offer edible flower petals to brighten up dishes and add a touch of floral sweetness.

- **Summer's Abundance:** Summer explodes with a riot of flavors. Juicy berries like blueberries, raspberries, and blackberries become the stars of jams, pies, and refreshing summer salads. Fragrant herbs like basil, oregano, and mint reach their peak, infusing dishes with their enriched aromas.

- **Autumn's Harvest:** As summer fades, autumn paints the landscape in fiery hues. Nut trees like walnuts and hazelnuts offer a bounty of protein-rich treats, while wild mushrooms emerge from the forest floor, adding a touch of earthy elegance to gourmet meals.

- **Winter's Quiet Bounty:** Even winter doesn't leave foragers empty-handed. Evergreens like spruce and pine offer vitamin-rich needles for teas, and some hardy mushrooms are found nestled beneath fallen logs.

Living in harmony with the seasons requires you to align your lifestyle with the earth's natural rhythm. You'll build a deeper appreciation for the ecosystem's delicate balance and encourage mindful consumption.

The Health Benefits of Foraging

Foraging is a way to nourish your body and soul. Here's how a foraging lifestyle can positively impact your health:

- **Fresh, Local Ingredients:** Foraged foods are inherently local and seasonal, offering a wealth of vitamins, minerals, and antioxidants when at their peak freshness, which translates to a more nutritious diet rich in the essential building blocks for optimal health.

- **Increased Physical Activity:** The act of foraging often involves spending time outdoors, walking through forests or fields. This leads to a more active outdoor life.

- **Stress Reduction:** Immersing yourself in nature is a proven stress reliever. The act of foraging allows you to disconnect from the hustle and bustle of daily life and find solace in the tranquility of the natural world.

- **A Sense of Accomplishment:** Successfully identifying and harvesting wild edibles brings accomplishment and self-reliance. It fosters a connection to your food source and a deeper appreciation for the natural world.

Foraging offers a holistic approach to well-being, nourishing your body with fresh, local ingredients while calming your mind and fostering accomplishment.

Environmental Benefits of Foraging

By embracing a foraging lifestyle, you contribute to a more sustainable future. Here's how:

- **Reduced Reliance on Processed Foods:** Foraged foods are a natural alternative to processed and packaged foods, often laden with artificial ingredients and excessive packaging. This translates to a lower carbon footprint and less waste.

- **Supporting Local Ecosystems:** Foraging encourages mindful harvesting practices, promoting healthy plant populations and fostering biodiversity within local ecosystems. By understanding sustainable harvesting techniques, you become a steward of the land, not a plunderer.

- **Appreciation for Conservation:** The act of foraging inspires a deeper appreciation for the natural world. You become invested in the health of local ecosystems, potentially moving you to get involved in conservation efforts or support organizations working to protect natural habitats.

Foraging is a gentle way to interact with the environment, promoting sustainable practices and fostering responsibility toward the delicate balance of nature.

Beyond the Pages of This Book

Your exploration of the foraging world doesn't end with the last page of this book. This newfound knowledge is a springboard for a lifelong journey of discovery and connection with the natural world. Here are some ways to keep the adventure going:

- **Seek Out Workshops and Classes:** Many organizations offer workshops and classes on foraging, wild plant identification, and sustainable harvesting practices. These programs provide opportunities to learn from experienced foragers, ask questions, and gain hands-on experience in a supportive environment.

- **Join a Foraging Group:** Consider connecting with local foraging clubs or online communities. Sharing your passion with like-minded individuals is a source of inspiration, education, and camaraderie. You can learn from each other's experiences, swap harvesting tips, and discover new forageable treasures in your area.

- **Become a Citizen Scientist:** Many organizations rely on citizen science programs to track plant populations and monitor the health of local ecosystems. Participating in these programs allows you to contribute valuable data while expanding your knowledge of the natural world.

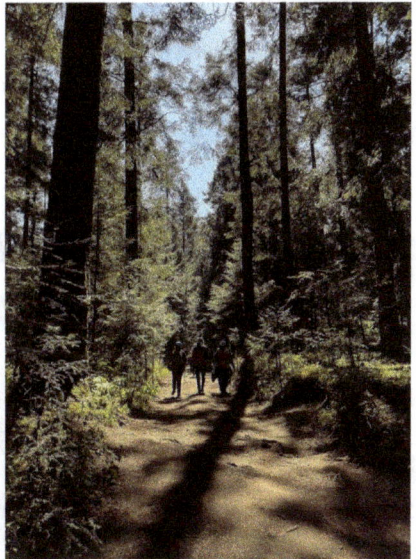

Join a foraging group.[66]

The best classroom is nature itself. Spend time outdoors, take notice of your surroundings, and be mindful of the changing seasons. Note the emerging spring greens, the summer berries, and the hidden treasures of the forest floor. With each passing year, your foraging skills will refine, and your connection with the natural world will deepen.

Integrating Foraged Bounty into Your Life

The true magic of foraging unfolds in the kitchen. Here are some tips for incorporating wild ingredients into your everyday meals:

- **Start Simple:** Begin by incorporating small amounts of foraged ingredients into familiar dishes. Wild greens are tossed into salads, while berries add a burst of flavor to yogurt or oatmeal. Experimentation is key, but start by adding familiar flavors to your existing culinary repertoire.

- **Embrace Seasonality:** Let the seasons guide your menu planning. Spring offers tender greens and vibrant flowers perfect for salads and light dishes. Summer explodes with juicy berries ideal for jams, pies, and refreshing drinks. Autumn brings a bounty of nuts and mushrooms, while winter offers opportunities to explore evergreen herbs and preserved harvests.

- **Preserve Your Bounty:** Learning basic preservation techniques allows you to enjoy the taste of the wild throughout the year. Drying, freezing, and pickling are excellent ways to extend the shelf life of your foraged finds. Explore resources and experiment with different preservation methods to create a pantry stocked with the wild flavors of each season.

Embrace the spirit of exploration in the kitchen. Research recipes specifically created using wild ingredients, or get inventive and make up your own new dishes. Allow the foraged flavors to inspire you, and don't be afraid to experiment with new taste combinations and culinary techniques.

Cultivating a Culture of Collaboration

The journey of a forager isn't a solitary pursuit. The knowledge you've gained isn't meant to be a closely guarded secret. It's a gift to be shared with others. By collaborating and sharing your passion for foraging, you contribute to your local community's collective wisdom and resilience. Here are some ways to share your newfound knowledge:

- **Become a Teacher:** Share your knowledge with friends and family. Organize casual foraging walks, teach them basic plant identification skills, and show them how to prepare simple dishes with wild ingredients. Inspiring others to connect with nature and appreciate the bounty of their local environment is a powerful way to spread the joy of foraging.

- **Engage in Community Events:** Many communities host events and workshops related to local food systems and sustainable living. Why not volunteer your skills at these events by leading foraging walks, demonstrating basic preparation techniques, or sharing recipes featuring wild ingredients? Sharing your knowledge in a public forum can inspire others and contribute to a more informed community.

- **Document Your Journey:** Keep a foraging journal to document your finds, note locations, and record successful recipes. Consider sharing your experiences online through blogs or social media platforms. You'll inspire others to start to explore foraging and contribute information to the collective knowledge base of the foraging community.

- **Support Local Initiatives:** Many organizations work to promote sustainable food systems, protect local ecosystems, and educate the public about the importance of wild plants. Consider volunteering your time or donating resources to these organizations. Supporting these initiatives ensures the continued availability of wild resources and encourages community responsibility towards the natural world.

Document your journey.[67]

Sharing your knowledge and experiences benefits others and also deepens your understanding. By teaching and discussing with others, you solidify your learning.

The act of foraging fosters a connection to the land, the seasons, and the community around you. By sharing your passion and knowledge, you contribute to a collective wisdom that empowers others to embrace a more sustainable and enriching way of life. As you continue your foraging journey, remember that the true reward lies in the bounty you harvest, the connections you make, and the knowledge you share along the way.

Following a Foraging Lifestyle

As you close this chapter, carry with you the spirit of exploration, the thrill of discovery, and a deep sense of connection cultivated on your foraging journey. More than just a way to find food, foraging is a philosophy that extends far beyond the boundaries of the forest floor. It's a call to embrace sustainability in all aspects of your life, a commitment to stewardship of the natural world, and a deep respect for the ecosystem's delicate balance.

Let the principles of foraging guide you. Reduce your reliance on processed foods, minimize your environmental impact, and become a conscious consumer. Advocate for sustainable practices in your community and support organizations dedicated to protecting local ecosystems.

Most importantly, continue foraging with wonder and an insatiable curiosity. Let the changing seasons ignite your passion, and allow the whispers of the wild to guide your exploration. Every new plant identification, every successful harvest, and every delicious dish prepared with foraged ingredients is a testament to the powerful connection you've forged with the natural world.

Foraging is not just about finding sustenance. It's about finding meaning, purpose, and fulfillment in your relationship with the Earth. It's about becoming an active participant in the symphony of nature, a steward of its bounty, and a storyteller of its wonders. So, lace up your boots, grab your basket, and venture forth with a sense of adventure and a heart brimming with respect for the wild world that awaits. The path less traveled, teeming with vivid life and hidden treasures, is yours to explore.

Bonus Section: Northeast Foraging Calendar

This bonus section is a visual guide to annual foraging opportunities in the Northeast. It's not an exhaustive list, and specific forage times may vary depending on your location and weather conditions.

Foraging Table

Northeast Foraging Calendar

This bonus section is a visual guide to annual foraging opportunities in the Northeast. It's not an exhaustive list, and specific forage times may vary depending on your location and weather conditions.

❄ Winter ／ 🌱 Spring ／ ☀ Summer ／ 🍁 Fall	Jan	Feb	Mar	Apr	May	Jun	Jul	Aug	Sep	Oct	Nov	Dec
WILD EDIBLES												
Morel Mushrooms			■	■	■							
Ramps				■	■							
Dandelion Greens			■	■	■							
Fiddleheads					■							
Wild Strawberries						■						
Blackberries							■	■				
Chanterelle Mushrooms							■	■	■	■		
Shagbark Hickory Nuts									■	■		
FUNGI												
Chicken of the Woods								▦	▦	▦		
Hedgehog Mushrooms									▦	▦	▦	
Hen of the Woods									▦	▦	▦	
Maitake Mushrooms										▦	▦	
Lobster Mushrooms								▦	▦	▦		
Black Trumpet							▦	▦	▦	▦		

MEDICINAL PLANTS

Yarrow									
Peppermint									
Goldenseal									
Echinacea									
Chamomile									

Index: A-Z of Wild Edibles, Fungi, and Medicinal Plants

Wild Edibles

- Blackberries (*Rubus* spp.) - Also known as brambleberries
- Blueberries (*Vaccinium* sect. *Cyanococcus*) - Also known as bilberries
- Butternuts (*Juglans cinerea*)
- Cranberries (*Vaccinium oxycoccos*) - Also known as bog cranberries, cowberries
- Dandelion Greens (*Taraxacum officinale*)
- Daylilies (*Hemerocallis spp.*) - Flowers only
- Elderflowers (*Sambucus nigra*)
- Fiddleheads (*Mattieuccia struthiopteris* and other species) - Young fronds of certain ferns
- Hazelnuts (*Corylus americana*) - Also known as cobnuts, filberts
- Nettles (*Urtica dioica*) - Wear gloves when handling
- Raspberries (*Rubus idaeus*) - Also known as framboise (French)
- Strawberries (*Fragaria* spp.) - Wild varieties may be smaller than cultivated ones
- Violets (*Viola* spp.) - Flowers and leaves of some varieties

- Walnuts (*Juglans nigra*) - Black walnuts
- Wild Garlic (*Allium canadense*) - Also known as wild onion or meadow garlic

Fungi

- Chanterelles (*Cantharellus* spp.) - Trumpet-shaped with yellow gills
- Chicken of the Woods (*Laetiporus sulphureus*) - Orange or yellow shelf-like clusters
- Hedgehog Mushrooms (*Hydnum repandum*) - Spines instead of gills on the underside of the cap
- Hen of the Woods (*Grifola frondosa*) - Clusters of fan-shaped or shelf-like caps
- Lion's Mane (*Hericium erinaceus*) - White, shaggy mushroom with teeth-like spines
- Maitake Mushrooms (*Grifola frondosa*) - Hen-of-the-woods mushrooms with clusters of gray-brown caps
- Morels (*Morchella* spp.) - Honeycomb-like caps with pits and ridges
- Oyster Mushrooms (*Pleurotus ostreatus*) - Fan-shaped caps with gills running down the stem

Medicinal Plants

- Bloodroot (*Sanguinaria canadensis*) - Topical use only under professional guidance
- Chamomile (*Matricaria recutita*) - Also known as German chamomile
- Echinacea (*Echinacea purpurea*) - Use ethically and sparingly
- Elderberry (*Sambucus nigra*) - Ripe berries only
- Goldenseal (*Hydrastis canadensis*) - Use ethically and sparingly, if at all
- Peppermint (*Mentha piperita*)
- Winterberry (*Ilex verticillata*) - Berries only; leaves and stems can cause nausea
- Witch Hazel (*Hamamelis virginiana*)

- Yarrow (*Achillea millefolium*) - Also known as milfoil

Toxic Plants and Fungi (Not for Consumption)

- American Black Nightshade (*Solanum americanum*) – Small, star-shaped white flowers with five conspicuous stamens in the center, followed by glossy red or black berries
- Red Elderberry (*Sambucus racemosa*) – Uncooked berries can cause nausea and vomiting
- Jack-o'-Lantern Mushroom (*Omphalotus olearius*) - Can cause severe stomach upset
- Poison Sumac (*Toxicodendron vernix*) - Causes severe skin irritation
- Poison Ivy (*Toxicodendron radicans*) - Causes severe skin irritation
- Poison Oak (*Toxicodendron diversilobum*) - Causes severe skin irritation

Note: *This is not an exhaustive list. Consult a reliable field guide and ensure proper identification before consuming any wild plant or fungus. When in doubt, always err on the side of caution and leave it out.*

If you enjoyed this book, I'd greatly appreciate a review on Amazon because it helps me to create more books that people want. It would mean a lot to hear from you.

To leave a review:

1. Open your camera app.
2. Point your mobile device at the QR code.
3. The review page will appear in your web browser.

_____

Thanks for your support!

Here's another book by Dion Rosser that you might like

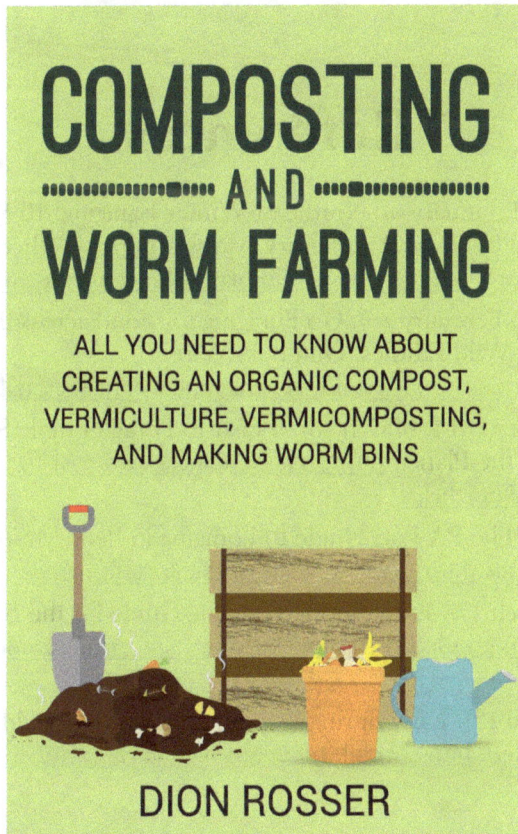

COMPOSTING
···············■···· AND ····■················
WORM FARMING

ALL YOU NEED TO KNOW ABOUT
CREATING AN ORGANIC COMPOST,
VERMICULTURE, VERMICOMPOSTING,
AND MAKING WORM BINS

DION ROSSER

References

Gardiner, B. (2024, January 6). Northeast Winter Foraging: 10 Wild Plants That You Can Eat - The Outdoor Apothecary. Www.outdoorapothecary.com. https://www.outdoorapothecary.com/wild-plants-that-you-can-eat/

Gleason, G. (2023, February 20). Go Foraging for Food across the US with This Regional Guide to Wild Edibles. Outdoors Wire. https://outdoorswire.usatoday.com/lists/foraging-food-us-regional-guide/

Joe@EatThePlanet. (2014, March 13). 5 Easy to Forage Edible Spring Plants of the Northeast. Eat the Planet. https://eattheplanet.org/5-easy-to-forage-edible-spring-plants-of-the-northeast/

Kovach, E. (n.d.). The PA Eats Guide to Foraging in Pennsylvania | Foraging Wild Foods. PA Eats. https://www.paeats.org/feature/foraging-in-pennsylvania/

Leslie. (2021, March 17). Early Spring Foraging Guide for the Northeast. PunkMed. https://punkmed.com/blog/early-spring-foraging-guide-for-the-northeast/

Leslie. (2024, April 12). Early Spring Foraging | Common Wild Edibles in the Northeast. PunkMed. https://punkmed.com/blog/early-spring-foraging/

Image Sources

[1] https://www.pexels.com/photo/pathway-between-green-leafed-trees-109391/

[2] DThompson1313, CC BY-SA 4.0 <https://creativecommons.org/licenses/by-sa/4.0>, via Wikimedia Commons. https://commons.wikimedia.org/wiki/File:Sean_Sherman_of_the_Company_The_Sioux_Chef_foraging_Wild_Ramps.jpg

[3] Aznaturalist, CC BY-SA 3.0 <https://creativecommons.org/licenses/by-sa/3.0>, via Wikimedia Commons. https://commons.wikimedia.org/wiki/File:BeachPlums.jpg

[4] https://www.pexels.com/photo/green-plant-close-up-photography-1098973/

[5] https://www.pexels.com/photo/bees-on-purple-flower-164470/

[6] https://www.pexels.com/photo/woman-in-stripe-dress-shirt-holding-radish-4894620/

[7] Matěj Baťha, CC BY-SA 2.5 <https://creativecommons.org/licenses/by-sa/2.5>, via Wikimedia Commons. https://commons.wikimedia.org/wiki/File:Pocket-knife_2.jpg

[8] Jeremy Noble, CC BY 2.0 <https://creativecommons.org/licenses/by/2.0>, via Wikimedia Commons. https://commons.wikimedia.org/wiki/File:Picnic_basket_01.jpg

[9] https://commons.wikimedia.org/wiki/File:Magnifying_Glass_Photo.jpg

[10] https://commons.wikimedia.org/wiki/File:ARS-habanero.jpg

[11] Arne Nordmann (norro), CC BY-SA 2.5 <https://creativecommons.org/licenses/by-sa/2.5>, via Wikimedia Commons. https://commons.wikimedia.org/wiki/File:Bear_attack_deterrent_spray.jpg

[12] Cactus26, CC BY-SA 3.0 <http://creativecommons.org/licenses/by-sa/3.0/>, via Wikimedia Commons. https://commons.wikimedia.org/wiki/File:TrekkingPolesCarbonWoman.jpg

[13] Auckland Museum, CC BY 4.0 <https://creativecommons.org/licenses/by/4.0>, via Wikimedia Commons. https://commons.wikimedia.org/wiki/File:Kit,_sewing_(AM_1965.78.588-8).jpg

[14] Nicholas A. Tonelli from Northeast Pennsylvania, USA, CC BY 2.0 <https://creativecommons.org/licenses/by/2.0>, via Wikimedia Commons

https://commons.wikimedia.org/wiki/File:Erie_National_Wildlife_Refuge_(Revisited)_(6)_(906254 1670).jpg

[15] https://www.pexels.com/photo/fiddlehead-in-macro-shot-photography-13079522/

[16] https://commons.wikimedia.org/wiki/File:Morel_mushroom_(6189023611).jpg

[17] Fungus Guy, CC BY-SA 3.0 <https://creativecommons.org/licenses/by-sa/3.0>, via Wikimedia Commons. https://commons.wikimedia.org/wiki/File:Wild_leeks_(Whitefish_I)_1.JPG

[18] George F Mayfield, CC BY-SA 2.0 <https://creativecommons.org/licenses/by-sa/2.0>, via Wikimedia Commons https://commons.wikimedia.org/wiki/File:Allium_canadense_WILD_ONION.jpg

[19] Violetcabra, CC0, via Wikimedia Commons https://commons.wikimedia.org/wiki/File:Young_Nettles_Shoots.jpg

[20] xulescu_g, CC BY-SA 2.0 <https://creativecommons.org/licenses/by-sa/2.0>, via Wikimedia Commons https://commons.wikimedia.org/wiki/File:Fragaria_vesca_(41503723130).jpg

[21] Dominicus Johannes Bergsma, CC BY-SA 4.0 <https://creativecommons.org/licenses/by-sa/4.0>, via Wikimedia Commons. https://commons.wikimedia.org/wiki/File:Opengebarsten_vrucht_van_beuk_(Fagus_sylvatica)_(d.j.b.)_02.jpg

[22] Photo by and (c)2007 Derek Ramsey (Ram-Man), GFDL 1.2 <http://www.gnu.org/licenses/old-licenses/fdl-1.2.html>, via Wikimedia Commons. https://commons.wikimedia.org/wiki/File:Swamp_Milkweed_Asclepias_incarnata_Flowers_Closeu p_2800px.jpg

[23] https://www.pexels.com/photo/selective-focus-photography-of-sunflower-1454288/

[24] Whut, CC BY-SA 3.0 <https://creativecommons.org/licenses/by-sa/3.0>, via Wikimedia Commons. https://commons.wikimedia.org/wiki/File:Eruca_sativa.jpg

[25] https://www.pexels.com/photo/close-up-of-american-branberrybush-9834623/

[26] https://www.pexels.com/photo/red-round-fruits-on-branches-9802366/

[27] https://www.pexels.com/photo/crop-unrecognizable-gardener-touching-lush-potted-rosemary-5967853/

[28] claralieu, CC BY 2.0 <https://creativecommons.org/licenses/by/2.0>, via Wikimedia Commons. https://commons.wikimedia.org/wiki/File:Grey_Oyster_Mushroom_-4.jpg

[29] Melissa McMasters from Memphis, TN, United States, CC BY 2.0 <https://creativecommons.org/licenses/by/2.0>, via Wikimedia Commons. https://commons.wikimedia.org/wiki/File:Lion%27s_mane_mushroom_(25639625671).jpg

[30] Sinisa Radic, CC BY-SA 4.0 <https://creativecommons.org/licenses/by-sa/4.0>, via Wikimedia Commons. https://commons.wikimedia.org/wiki/File:Grifola_frondosa_03.jpg

[31] Tourism NT, Attribution, via Wikimedia Commons. https://commons.wikimedia.org/wiki/File:Australian_bush_tucker,_Alice_Springs.jpg

[32] https://www.pexels.com/photo/dandelion-grayscale-photography-21323/

[33] Björn S..., CC BY-SA 2.0 <https://creativecommons.org/licenses/by-sa/2.0>, via Wikimedia Commons. https://commons.wikimedia.org/wiki/File:Peronospora_variabilis_on

 Lamb%27s_Quarters_-_Chenopodium_album_(31548634888).jpg

[34] https://www.pexels.com/photo/selective-focus-of-blooming-chickweed-flowers-12167043/

[35] Cbaile19, CC0, via Wikimedia Commons
https://commons.wikimedia.org/wiki/File:Viola_sororia,_2023-05-05,_Kane_Woods,_05.jpg

[36] W. Bulach, CC BY-SA 4.0 <https://creativecommons.org/licenses/by-sa/4.0>, via Wikimedia
Commons. https://commons.wikimedia.org/wiki/File:00_3775_Schwarzer
Hollunder(Sambucus_nigra).jpg

[37] Jeangagnon, CC BY-SA 4.0 <https://creativecommons.org/licenses/by-sa/4.0>, via Wikimedia
Commons https://commons.wikimedia.org/wiki/File:Hemerocallis_-_2024-06-28.jpg

[38] Σ64, CC BY 3.0 <https://creativecommons.org/licenses/by/3.0>, via Wikimedia Commons
https://upload.wikimedia.org/wikipedia/commons/0/01/Vaccinium_angustifolium_04.jpg

[39] https://www.pexels.com/photo/red-raspberry-52536/

[40] https://www.pexels.com/photo/blackberries-on-table-892808/

[41] Dcrjsr, CC BY 4.0 <https://creativecommons.org/licenses/by/4.0>, via Wikimedia Commons
https://commons.wikimedia.org/wiki/File:Quercus_alba_2-acorn_branch.jpg

[42] Alina Zienowicz Ala z, CC BY-SA 3.0 <https://creativecommons.org/licenses/by-sa/3.0>, via
Wikimedia Commons
https://commons.wikimedia.org/wiki/File:Quercus_rubra_2008_07_06_%281%29.JPG

[43] EgorovaSvetlana, CC BY-SA 4.0 <https://creativecommons.org/licenses/by-sa/4.0>, via
Wikimedia Commons https://commons.wikimedia.org/wiki/File:Hickory_Tree_
Carya_ovata_Arnold_Arboretum.jpg

[44] Plant Image Library from Boston, USA, CC BY-SA 2.0
<https://creativecommons.org/licenses/by-sa/2.0>, via Wikimedia Commons
https://commons.wikimedia.org/wiki/File:Juglans_nigra_%28Black_Walnut%29_14761%2AA_%28
37484739526%29.jpg

[45] Agnieszka Kwiecień, Nova, CC BY-SA 4.0 <https://creativecommons.org/licenses/by-sa/4.0>, via
Wikimedia Commons. https://commons.wikimedia.org/wiki/File:Arctium_lappa_
%C5%81opian_wi%C4%99kszy_2023-07-30_05.jpg

[46] Dietmar Rabich / Wikimedia Commons / "Münster, Botanischer Garten – 2016 -- 3871" /
CC BY-SA 4.0For print products: Dietmar Rabich /
https://commons.wikimedia.org/wiki/File:M%C3%BCnster,_Botanischer_Garten_–_2016_--
_3871.jpg / https://creativecommons.org/licenses/by-sa/4.0/.
https://commons.wikimedia.org/wiki/File:M%C3%BCnster,_Botanischer_Garten_–_2016_--
_3871.jpg

[47] Miscellaneous contributor, CC0, via Wikimedia Commons.
https://commons.wikimedia.org/wiki/File:Wild_carrot_flower_(Daucus_carota).jpg

[48] Jim Champion / Fungi growing on a pine stump, Frame Heath Inclosure, New Forest.
https://commons.wikimedia.org/wiki/File:Fungi_growing_on_a_pine_stump,_Frame_Heath_Inclos
ure,_New_Forest_-_geograph.org.uk_-_261258.jpg

---

[49] debivort, CC BY-SA 3.0 <https://creativecommons.org/licenses/by-sa/3.0>, via Wikimedia Commons. https://commons.wikimedia.org/wiki/File:Mushroom_cap_morphology2.png

[50] Treetale, CC BY 3.0 <https://creativecommons.org/licenses/by/3.0>, via Wikimedia Commons. https://commons.wikimedia.org/wiki/File:Jack_O%27_Lantern_Mushroom_Closeup;_Omphalotus_olearius.JPG

[51] Netherzone, CC BY-SA 4.0 <https://creativecommons.org/licenses/by-sa/4.0>, via Wikimedia Commons. https://commons.wikimedia.org/wiki/File:Chanterelles_foraged_in_the_Rocky_Mountains.jpg

[52] Chiring Chandan, CC BY-SA 4.0 <https://creativecommons.org/licenses/by-sa/4.0>, via Wikimedia Commons. https://commons.wikimedia.org/wiki/File:Pleurotus_ostreatus_(Oyster_Mushroom)_1.jpg

[53] Susan Slater, CC BY-SA 4.0 <https://creativecommons.org/licenses/by-sa/4.0>, via Wikimedia Commons. https://commons.wikimedia.org/wiki/File:39_-_IMG_20150712_143214.jpg

[54] https://www.pexels.com/photo/pyracantha-coccinea-tree-with-red-berries-4425014/

[55] Chris 論, CC BY 3.0 <https://creativecommons.org/licenses/by/3.0>, via Wikimedia Commons. https://commons.wikimedia.org/wiki/File:Vogel-Sternmieren-Salat.jpg

[56] https://www.pexels.com/photo/stuffed-grape-leaves-6089620/

[57] https://www.pexels.com/photo/blueberries-jam-in-jar-4963906/

[58] https://www.pexels.com/photo/bowl-of-pasta-with-asparagus-and-parmesan-11929430/

[59] https://www.pexels.com/photo/dried-flowers-in-glass-jar-20862425/

[60] https://www.pexels.com/photo/shallow-focus-photography-of-yellow-and-white-flowers-during-daytime-159110/

[61] I, KENPEI, CC BY-SA 3.0 <http://creativecommons.org/licenses/by-sa/3.0/>, via Wikimedia Commons. https://commons.wikimedia.org/wiki/File:Melissa_officinalis2.jpg

[62] Ulf Eliasson, CC BY-SA 3.0 <http://creativecommons.org/licenses/by-sa/3.0/>, via Wikimedia Commons. https://commons.wikimedia.org/wiki/File:EchinaceaPurpureaMaxima1a.UME.JPG

[63] Agnieszka Kwiecień (Nova), CC BY-SA 3.0 <https://creativecommons.org/licenses/by-sa/3.0>, via Wikimedia Commons. https://commons.wikimedia.org/wiki/File:Sambucus_nigra-fruit001.jpg

[64] https://www.myupchar.com/en, CC BY-SA 4.0 <https://creativecommons.org/licenses/by-sa/4.0>, via Wikimedia Commons. https://commons.wikimedia.org/wiki/File:Depiction_of_a_person_suffering_from_Allergic_Rhinitis.png

[65] Abuluntu, CC BY-SA 4.0 <https://creativecommons.org/licenses/by-sa/4.0>, via Wikimedia Commons. https://commons.wikimedia.org/wiki/File:Collage_forage_wikibooks.jpg

[66] https://www.pexels.com/photo/people-on-a-path-in-a-forest-20876843/

[67] https://www.pexels.com/photo/person-writing-on-red-notebook-261735/

www.ingramcontent.com/pod-product-compliance
Lightning Source LLC
Chambersburg PA
CBHW071941260326
41914CB00004B/714